English Code 2

Student's Book

Contents

Values	Phonics	STEAM	Language lab 2	Project and Review
Listen to your friends.	a, e bag, cap, cat, man, mat, pan, clap leg, pen, peg, pet, ten, wet	**Engineering:** Building materials **Experiment:** Building a strong tower	**Language Lab 2** There's a river. There are houses. There isn't a park. There aren't any farms.	Make a town guide.
Be prepared.	i, o bin, dig, hit, sing, sit, six dog, fox, hop, hot, jog, frog, stop	**Science:** Space systems: the sun and earth **Experiment:** Finding out how the earth and sun move	**Language Lab 2** He eats three bananas. He doesn't eat apples. Does he eat bananas? Yes, he does. No, he doesn't.	Do a day and night presentation.
Help people in need.	u, x bug, jug, nut, rug, run, sun ax, box, fox, ox, six, taxi	**Science:** Solids and liquids **Experiment:** Recording how some liquids change	**Language Lab 2** Our box is yellow. Ours is yellow. Their box is pink. Theirs is pink.	Create a class museum.
Ask people before you take photos.	j, y jacket, jaguar, jar, jeans, jog, juice, jump, jungle yak, yellow, yes, yo-yo, yogurt, you, young, yours	**Art and design:** Facial expressions: changing faces **Experiment:** Recording how we change and react to others' emotions and expressions	**Language Lab 2** Do you have a brother? Yes, I do. He's funny! Do you have a sister? No, I don't.	Create a portrait gallery.
Be kind. Ask people what they like and don't like.	ch, sh chair, cheese, cherries, chess, chicken, chips sheep, shelf, ship, shirt, shoes, shop, shorts	**Technology:** Milk processes **Experiment:** Making ice cream	**Language Lab 2** Can I have this salad, please? Can I have that salad, please?	Create a class meal. Pasta, chicken, and cheese Ice cream and mango Grapes and watermelon
I share my skills and help my friends to do things.	th that, there, these, they, this, those thank, things, thirteen, three, throw	**Maths:** Measurement **Experiment:** Measuring the air in our lungs	**Language Lab 2** Can you ride a bike? Yes, I can. No, I can't.	Organize a Sports Day.
Respond kindly and with interest.	wh, f fan, farm, fat, fish, five, funny what, wheel, when, where, which, white	**Science:** Biodegradable trash **Experiment:** Recording how long biodegradable and non-biodegradble materials take to change	**Language Lab 2** Whose house is it? It's Amy's house.	Design a dream house.
Show concern for each other.	s, sh, j, ch soup, sun, see shell, shoe, shop jeep, juice, jump cheese, cherry, chicken	**Science:** Landforms: mountains **Experiment:** Making mountains with towels	**Language Lab 2** above, behind, in, in front of, near, next to, on, opposite, under	Make a nature scrapbook.

Welcome!

How can I talk about myself?

1 What do you do at your school? Circle and say.

2 002 💬 **Listen and point. Then chant.**

Monday   Tuesday   Wednesday   Thursday

Friday   Saturday   Sunday

3 003 **Listen, sing along, and dance.**

Monday

SONG 🎵 TIME 🎵

Good morning!

Good morning, children!
How are you? It's **Monday** today!
We're at school and we can sing
And read and write and play!

Good morning, teacher!
We are fine! It's Monday today!
We're at school and we can sing
And read and write and play!

*We're at school, we're at school,
We're at school today! X4*

read!

write!

Months and seasons
VOCABULARY

I will learn months and seasons words.

1 🎧 004 Listen, point, and repeat. Then chant!

January February March April May June

July August September October November December

2 🎧 005 💬 Listen, point, and repeat. Then complete the pictures.

The four seasons

spring

summer

fall

winter

3 💬 Work with a partner. Say the season.

December!

December is in _____ !

4 ✦ Make a calendar. Work in groups.

Language lab 1

GRAMMAR: I'M / I AM

I will talk about how old I am using **I am … / You are … / He is …**

1 ▶ 🎧 006 Watch. Then read, and check ☑.

 a
 b
 a
 b

1 He's a bird.   2 She's a frog.

I'm = I am	
You're = You are	
He's = He is	
She's = She is	
It's = It is	
We're = We are	
They're = They are	

2 Write am, is, or are. Then circle.

 1   8
 2   9 9
 3   7 7

 4   10
 5   6

1   You're 8. You _____ three / eight .

2   We're 9. We _____ seven / nine .

3   They're 7. They _____ seven / five .

4   I'm 10. I _____ two / ten .

5   She's 6. She _____ six / one .

3 💬 Play the *He/She* game.

This is Emma. She's seven.

No, I'm eight!

Yes … she's eight.

4 ⚙ Make labels.

HE   SHE   HE   IT

Story lab
READING

1 007 **Read and listen. What is the teacher's name?**

Nice to meet you!

1 Good morning, children! My name is Miss Kelly. I'm your teacher. We're Class 2A.

Good morning, Miss Kelly!

2 What's your name?

I'm Leo!

How old are you?

I'm eight. I like books and cars!

3 I have a sister ... Anna!

How old is she?

She's seven.

4 Yes, I'm Anna and I'm seven.

Do you like cars and books?

Yes, I do! I like rabbits, too!

5 Hi! My name's Tom. I'm eight. I like frogs and lizards and cats!

2 Look at the story again. Choose and write.

Anna   books   eight (2)   frogs and lizards   Leo   rabbits   seven   Tom

1 **ID**

My name is _____ .
I'm _____ years old.
I like _____ and cars. My birthday is in July.

2 **ID**

My name is _____ .
I'm _____ years old.
I like _____ , books and cars. My birthday is in May.

3 **ID**

My name is _____ .
I'm _____ years old.
I like _____ and cats! My birthday is in April.

3 Play *Who am I?*

I'm eight. My birthday is in July.

You're Leo!

4 Make your own name card.

5 Act out the story in groups.

1 Out and about!

How can I create a town guide?

1 Where do you want to go in the town?

2 Stick the items on the places in the town.

3 Where can you find these things? Point and say.

CODE CRACKER

4 008 Listen and point. Then sing along and dance.

SONG TIME

Here, there, everywhere!

here!

*I like it here, I like it there,
I like it, like it everywhere!*

There are **stores** and there's a **school**.
There's a **castle** and a **pool**!

*I like it here, I like it there,
I like it, like it everywhere!*

Where are they?

VOCABULARY

I will learn town words.

1 🎧 009 **Listen, point, and repeat.**

1 house

2 store

3 library

4 farm

5 museum

6 playground

7 park

8 café

9 river

10 swimming pool

11 castle

12 school

2 🎧 010 💡 **Listen and circle.**

1 school / playground

2 café / castle

3 farm / museum

4 river / store

3 💬 **Look at 1. Circle the places you like. Then say.**

I like the park!

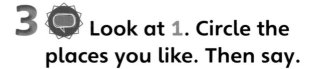

I like the swimming pool and the farm!

4 Mom is busy today! Read, draw, and number.

CODE CRACKER

Go to the ...

1 park   2 library

3 farm   4 store

5 school

5 Where are they? Write.

1   farm

2 _____

3 _____

4 _____

5 _____

6 _____

6 Where can you do these things? Write. Then say.

1 play _____

2 eat and drink _____

3 climb _____

4 swim _____

> I can swim in a swimming pool.

> I can eat and drink in a café.

7 Make your own picture dictionary. Draw and write town words.

_____castle_____   _____park_____

Language lab 1

GRAMMAR 1: LIKE / DON'T LIKE

I will talk about town words using **like / don't like**.

1  Watch. What does Milly like? Check ☑ or cross ☒.

> I **like** parks. 😃
> I **don't like** stores. 🙁
> Does she **like** playgrounds?
> Yes, she does. / No, she doesn't.
> He **likes** parks.
> She **doesn't like** stores.

Milly likes …

2 Watch again and circle.

1   Anna likes / doesn't like clothes stores.

2   Milly likes / doesn't like cars.

3 Read and draw 😃 or 🙁.

1   I don't like castles. ◯

2   Leo doesn't like stores. ◯

3   Milly likes farms. ◯

4   I like museums. ◯

4 Plan a day out with a partner. Ask and answer. Then write.

 a
 b
 c

> Do you like parks?

> Yes, I do.

> Do you like park a?

> No, I don't. I like park b.

1 I like park _____ *b* .

2 I don't like _____ .

3 My partner likes _____ .

4 My partner doesn't like _____ .

> Do you like swimming pools?

 a
 b
 c

1 I _____ swimming pool _____ .

2 I don't _____ swimming pool _____ .

3 My partner _____ swimming pool _____ .

4 My partner doesn't _____ swimming pool _____ .

5 Which places do you like? Write for you and your partner. Now decide. Where do you want to go?

CODE CRACKER

	Me	My partner	Our choice
Park			
Pool			

6 Now talk about your choice.

> I like park a. Carla likes park c.

> We both like swimming pool c!

Values Listen to your friends.

7 How do you and your friends decide what to do? Check ☑ the correct box.

1 I only do what I want to do. ☐

2 I listen to my friends and we decide together. ☐

Story lab

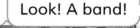

I will read a story about a town.

1 012 Read and listen. Why is it a special day in Castle Town?

A special day

1

Listen, Anna! I can hear music!

What's happening, Leo?

I don't know!

2

Look! A band!

Wow! The town is beautiful today!

3

I like the castle!

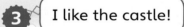

It's red and yellow!

4

Oh, no! Look, Anna!

Help! I can't stop!

2 Look at the story. Then match and number.

1 Anna

2 Leo

3 Miss Kelly

4 Castle Town

16 sixteen

5 Thank you!

You're welcome!

6 Good morning, Miss Kelly!

Good morning! Come into school. Where are Anna and Leo?

7 We're here, Miss Kelly!

We have a big cake!

Happy birthday, Castle Town!

3 Look at the story again. Then read and circle.

1   It plays music.   a band / the school

2   It's red and yellow.   the museum / the castle

3   It's 100 years old!   Castle Town / Miss Kelly

4 What makes the castle red and yellow today? Check ☑.

5 Act out the story in groups.

Phonics lab

> I will learn the **a** and **e** sounds.

1 013 Listen and repeat. Then write a or e.

1 c ____ p   **2** b ____ g   **3** m ____ t   **4** p ____ g   **5** t ____ n   **6** p ____ t

2 014 Listen and chant.

A **man** and a **pan**.

Cats on a **mat**.

Ten pets.

Oh no! Oh no!

Ten wet pets!

3 015 Listen and play the game.

a = clap   e = hop on one leg

4 Look and match.

Experiment lab

ENGINEERING: HOW TO BUILD A HOUSE

I will learn about building materials.

 Watch a video about buildings

1  **What do we need to build a house? Check ☑ or cross ☒.**

1 bricks   2 wood   3 cement

4 straws   5 steel   6 spaghetti

2 **016** **Now listen, read, and check your answers.**

Houses are made of cement and bricks and steel. There is wood in this house, too. This house is strong.

3 **Which house is strong? Look and circle a or b.**

a   b

EXPERIMENT TIME

How can I build a tower?

Look! This is the Eiffel Tower.

1 **Build a tower.**

You need:
spaghetti
clay

You need:
cups
construction paper

2 **Can you put books on your tower? Is it strong? Circle.**

	Spaghetti tower	Cups tower
I can put books on my tower.	Yes / No	Yes / No
My tower is strong.	Yes / No	Yes / No

Language lab 2

I will describe places using **there is / there are**.

There's a river. 😀

There are houses. 😐

There isn't a playground. 🙁

There aren't any farms. 🙁

There is = There's

1 🎧 017 Listen and read.

We're at a miniature village.
There are houses. There's a river.
There are stores. There's a castle.
There isn't a farm. There's a
school. There aren't any museums.
There are three cafés.

2 Now write about your town.

1 There _____ a school.

2 There _____ a castle.

3 There _____ houses.

4 There _____ museums.

3 Look, count, add, and write.

MATH ZONE

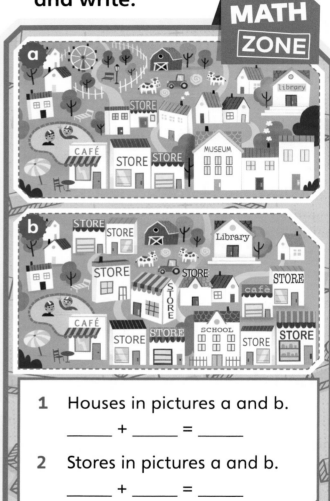

1 Houses in pictures a and b.
   _____ + _____ = _____

2 Stores in pictures a and b.
   _____ + _____ = _____

4 💬 Which picture is it? Ask and answer.

Are there any houses?

Yes! There are eleven houses.

Picture a!

Let's play!

COMMUNICATION

I will talk about games.

Let's make a castle.

Good idea!

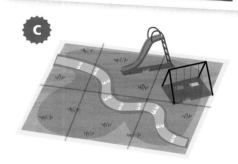

1 **Which game is it? Listen and write a, b, or c.**

1 _____   2 _____   3 _____

a Build a town

This game has six houses four stores a castle

b

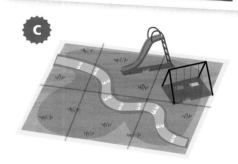
c

2 **Think about your favorite game. Talk about it with a partner using these words.**

Let's play …   This is my favorite.
Me, too.   OK.   It's great.
There is/isn't/are/aren't …

Let's play with the farm.

OK!

3 **Design a game. Draw and write.**

My game is _____.

There's a/an _____.

There are _____.

There isn't/aren't any _____.

4 **Now tell the class about your game.**

Do you like my game? Look … there's a school, a river …

PROJECT AND REVIEW

Make a town guide

Step 1

Research

 What's in my town?

- ☐ Think about your favorite places.
- ☐ Find photos.
- ☐ Find information and write notes.

What are my favorite places?

pool
library

Step 2

Plan

 What will you do?

- ☐ Plan a town guide.
- ☐ Read my notes.
- ☐ Choose places in my town.
- ☐ Draw or take photos of places in my town.

Step 3

Create

 How can I create my town guide?

- [ ] Design your page(s).
- [ ] Write about your town.
- [ ] Decorate your page(s).
- [ ] Check your work.

My favorite place is the swimming pool!

Step 4

Show and tell

Present your guide.

- [ ] Talk to friends about your town.
- [ ] Are any places missing?

Look, this is my house.

And this is the castle.

My Town
My House

There is a big castle.

Show a new friend around your town.

Now I can ...

... use town words.

... talk about my town using **like / don't like**.

... describe places and things using **there is / there are**.

2 Day and night

1 💬 **Point and say,** It's day/It's night.

2 💡 **When do they wake up? Stick the animals on the picture.**

3 💡 **Who am I? Check ☑ or cross ☒.**

CODE CRACKER

1	I'm brown.	☐	☐	☐
2	… and I have four legs.	☐	☐	☐
3	… and I play at night.	☐	☐	☐
4	I'm a/an	☐	☐	☐

4 🎧 019 **Listen and point. Then sing along and dance.**

SONG 🎵 TIME

Wonderful things

wake up!

In the day, in the day, I **wake up**,
And la, la, la, I sing!
At night, at night, I **sleep**,
And dream of wonderful things.

sing!

La, la, la, I sing
La, la, la, I sing
La, la, la, I sing
I dream of wonderful things!

twit twoo

At night, at night, the owl wakes up,
And twit, twit, twoo, he sings!
In the day, in the day, he sleeps
And dreams of wonderful things.

sleep!

What is it?

VOCABULARY

I will learn animal and daily routine words.

1 🎧 020 💬 Listen, point, and repeat.

 **1** cow

 **2** goat

 **3** donkey

 **4** owl

 **5** porcupine

 **6** bat

 **7** eat

 **8** wake up

 **9** sleep

 **10** brush my teeth

 **11** wash my face

 **12** go to school

2 Label the pictures. Use the words and phrases in 1.

1 ___bat___   **2** _____

3 _____   **4** _____

1 ___sleep___   **2** _____

3 _____   **4** _____

Values Be prepared.

3 When do you need these things? Circle.

When I ...

1	2	3	4
brush my teeth / wash my face	eat / sleep	go to school / wake up	wake up / eat

4 Check ☑ or cross ☒.

Which animal has ...

	four legs	two legs	big ears
cow			
goat			
owl			
donkey			
bat			
porcupine			

5 Now play *Guess the animal.*

It has four legs and big ears.

A donkey!

6 Make your own picture dictionary. Draw and write animal and daily routine words.

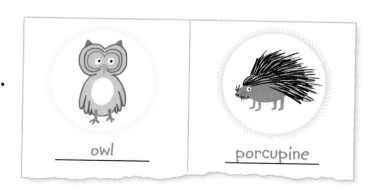

owl

porcupine

Language lab 1

I will talk about daily routines.

1 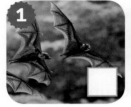  **Watch. What is Leo talking about? Check ☑ the correct picture.**

2 **What do *you* think owls say? Write the sound.**

Owls say _____

3 **What do you and your friends do at school? Check ☑ or cross ☒. Then write We …/We don't … .**

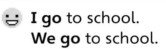
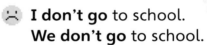
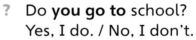

☺ **I go** to school.
We go to school.

☹ **I don't go** to school.
We don't go to school.

? Do **you go to** school?
Yes, I do. / No, I don't.

☐ eat   ☐ sleep

☐ play   ☐ sing

☐ brush our teeth   ☐ read

At school …

1   We _____

2   _____

3   _____

4   _____

5   _____

6   _____

4  **Choose and complete the questions. Circle _Yes_ or _No_. Then listen and check.**

> brush   wash   eat   sleep   wake   swim

Quiz Time!

1 Do cats _____ their faces?

Yes   No

Do you _____ your face?

_____

2 Do porcupines _____ in rivers?

Yes   No

Do you _____ in rivers?

_____

3 Do bats _____ at night?

Yes   No

Do you _____ at night?

_____

4 Do cows _____ their teeth?

Yes   No

Do you _____ your teeth?

_____

5 Do goats _____ grass?

Yes   No

Do you _____ grass?

_____

6 Do donkeys _____ up in the morning?

Yes   No

Do you _____ in the morning?

_____

5 Look at 4 again and write answers for you.

6 **Play _True or False_ with a partner.**

Goats don't eat grass.

False!

I brush my teeth.

True!

Story lab
READING

I will read a story about farm animals.

1 🔧 (023) Read and listen. What farm animals can you see?

Do goats dance?

1 Look, girls and boys. This is a cow. It eats grass.

3 This is a goat. Goats eat grass and fruit.

2 Do cows sing, Miss Kelly?

No, Tom! They don't sing. They say "moo!"

4 Do goats dance, Miss Kelly?

No, Tom! They don't dance!

2 🔧 Look at the story. Read and circle T (True) or F (False).

1 Miss Kelly is a teacher.   T / F

2 They go to Mrs. Hay's farm.   T / F

3 The cow doesn't like the song.   T / F

4 Mrs. Hay's animals dance and sing.   T / F

3 🔧 💬 Match. Then say who is speaking.

1 On the ●——   ●a happening?

2 What's ●——   ●b bus!

3 I don't ●——   ●c girls and boys.

4 Look, ●——   ●d know!

What's happening?

Miss Kelly is speaking.

5 On the bus!

To Mrs. Hay's farm, please!

6 Hello, Mrs. Hay. What's happening?

I don't know!

7 They like the music! They like this song!

8 Miss Kelly ... cows sing and goats dance!

Yes, Tom!

4 Where do the animals go? Look at the animal footprints and write go or don't go.

1 The cats _____ to the house.

2 The cats _____ to the park.

3 The donkeys _____ to the house.

4 The donkeys _____ to the park.

5 Act out the story in groups.

Phonics lab

I will learn the i and o sounds.

1 🎧 024 Listen and repeat. Then write i or o.

1 d ___ g   **2** b ___ n   **3** h ___ t

4 f ___ x   **5** j ___ g   **6** h ___ t

2 🎧 025 💬 Listen and chant.

Sit and **sing**,
Sit and **sing**,
Six little children **sit** and **sing**!

Jog, jog, jog!
Hop, hop, hop!
Stop!
The **dog** and the **frog** are **hot, hot, hot!**

3 🎧 026 💬 Listen and play the game. Jump to i or o!

4 Trace and match.

1

2

3

i   o

4

5

6

Experiment lab

SCIENCE: THE SUN AND THE EARTH

I will learn about the earth and the sun.

1 **Listen and read. Look at the pictures and write 1–4.**

1   We see the sun in the sky. It's day.

2   The sun shines on the earth.

3   The earth goes round and round in 24 hours. That is a day.

4   The earth goes around the sun in 12 months. That is a year.

It's night.   It's day.

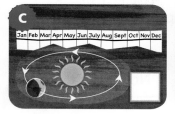

2 **Circle T (True) or F (False).**

1   We see the earth in the sky.   T / F

2   There are 24 hours in a day.   T / F

3   There are 12 months in a year.   T / F

12 hours day + 12 hours night = 24 hours.
We say "a day."

EXPERIMENT TIME

How does the earth move?

1 **Make an earth and a sun.**

Make a green and blue ball. That is the earth.

Make a big yellow circle. That is the sun.

2 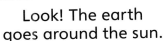 **Check ☑ and say.**

Look! The earth goes around the sun. ☐

Look! The sun goes around the earth. ☐

3 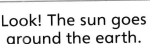 **Move your earth around the sun with a partner and say the sentence in 2 again.**

 Watch a video about space.

I will ask and answer about daily routines.

1 🔆 🎧028 **What's wrong? Correct the sentences. Then listen and check.**

He **eats** three bananas every day! 😃

He **doesn't eat** apples. 🙁

Does he eat bananas?

Yes, **he does**. 😃

No, **he doesn't**. 🙁

CODE CRACKER

1 He **eats** coconuts every day.

No! _He doesn't eat coconuts_ !

2 It **reads** books every day.

No! _____ !

3 She **doesn't go** to school.

No! _____ !

4 He **doesn't wash** his face.

No! _____ !

2 💬 **Choose. Then ask and answer with a partner.**

read   eat an apple
go to the museum

Do you eat an apple every day?

No, I don't.

3 Write Yes, he does/No, he doesn't/Yes, she does/No, she doesn't.

1   Does your partner read every day?   _____

2   Does your partner eat an apple every day?   _____

3   Does your partner go to the museum every day?   _____

4 💬 **Now tell the class about your partner.**

Bella reads every day.

What time is it?

COMMUNICATION

I will ask and answer about time and daily routines.

1 Write the missing numbers on the clock.

eight   two   three   twelve   six   ten

MATH ZONE

eleven   one

nine

four

seven   five

2 What time do you do these things? Write the number below.

_____ o'clock   _____ o'clock   _____ o'clock

_____ o'clock   _____ o'clock   _____ o'clock

3 Ask and answer with a partner. Then tell the class.

Do you wake up at seven o'clock?

No, I don't. I wake up at six o'clock.

Does Katy wake up at seven o'clock?

No, she doesn't. She wakes up at six o'clock.

4 Play the game.

What time is it?

It's three o'clock!

PROJECT AND REVIEW

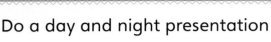

Do a day and night presentation

Step 1

Research

 How are day and night different?

- [ ] Write down a list of things that you see in the day.
- [ ] Write down a list of things that you see at night.
- [ ] Find out which animals sleep in the day and which sleep at night.
- [ ] Research why some animals sleep in the day and some at night.

Cows and goats sleep at night.

It's night. We can see the moon.

It's day. We can see the sun.

Step 2

Plan

 How can I plan my presentation?

- [ ] In teams, choose two things that are different in the day and at night.
- [ ] Choose one animal you want to talk about. Does it sleep in the day or at night? Why?
- [ ] Practice what to say.

Step 3

Create

 How can I create props?

- [ ] Make an animal mask.
- [ ] Make a sun and moon.
- [ ] Label your work.
- [ ] Make a poster for your presentation.

Step 4

Show and tell

 Share your day and night presentation with friends.

- [ ] Do a day and night presentation.
- [ ] Do animal movements.
- [ ] Talk about animals.

I'm an owl!

I don't sleep at night! Twit twoo!

Choose an animal. Find out more. Tell your friends.

Porcupines have big teeth! They eat wood!

Now I can ...

... use animal and daily routine words.

... talk about daily routines.

... ask and answer about daily routines.

1 🎧 029 **Listen and follow. Say the number.**

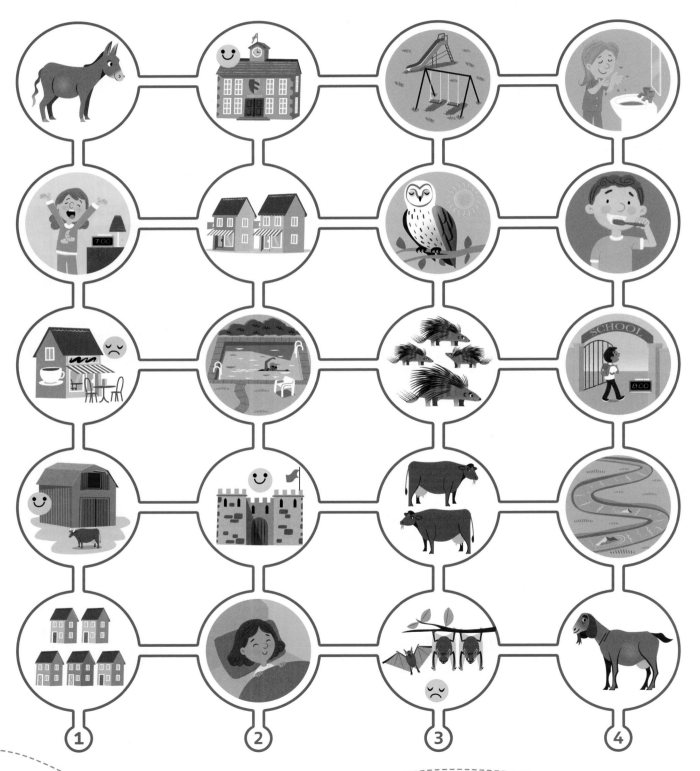

2 Read and follow. Draw the arrows. ← → ↑ ↓

1
1. There's a donkey. ○
   I like school! ○
   There are two stores. ○
   The owl sleeps in the day. ○
   Look at the playground!

2
2. I wash my face. ○
   He brushes his teeth. ○
   He goes to school at eight o'clock. ○
   There's a river. ○
   There are two cows.

3 Follow the arrows and write.

sleep   brushes   go   don't   are   cows   is   goat   like   pool

1
1. He _____ his teeth. ↓
   I _____ to school at eight o'clock. ←
   There _____ four porcupines. ↓
   There are two _____ . →
   There _____ a river.

2
2. There is a brown _____ . ←
   I _____ like bats. ←
   I _____ at night. ↑
   I _____ castles. ↑
   There is a _____ .

4 Ask and answer with a partner.

How many houses are there?

There are five houses.

Long nights, long days

CULTURE

1 Look at the pictures. What animals can you see? Say.

2 🎧 030 Listen and read.

I'm Hugo. I live in Sweden.

This is my town, Kiruna.

Kiruna is in the Arctic.

My house is made of wood.

Look at the blue, green, and purple lights!

In December, I go to school at eight o'clock, and I see the moon. I go home at three o'clock, and I see the moon!

The moon is in the sky all day and all night!

There are elks and bears in my country.

The bears sleep in December.

Fun Fact!

We swim in the river at night!

In June, I go to bed at nine o'clock, and the sun is in the sky. The sun is in the sky all day and all night!

This is Antarctica.

In December, the sun is in the sky all day and all night!

In June, the moon is in the sky all night and all day!

There are elephant seals in Antarctica.

Elephant seals have big noses. They eat fish.

3 Read again. Then draw a sun or a moon.

	December (night and day)	June (night and day)
The Arctic		
Antarctica		

4 Talk to a partner and guess.

There are elks and bears.

Sweden!

My Culture

Find out about the animals in your country.

5 Make an animal map.

6 Talk about the animals on your map.

Pandas eat leaves.

They sleep in the day and night!

3 Lost and found

How can I make a class museum?

1 🗨 **What can you see? Point and say.**

2 ⚙ **Stick, and write the colors and the shape on the picture.**

ball   bird   book

3 What do you think this is? Check ☑.

CODE CRACKER

1 a dog ☐
2 a cat ☐
3 a goat ☐

4 🎧 031 Listen and point. Then sing along and dance.

SONG TIME 🎵🎵

What does it look like? 🎵

What does it look like? *X4*
Is it **round**?
No, no!
Is it brown?
No, no!

What does it look like? *X4*
Is it **new**?
No, no!
Is it blue?
No, no, no!

What does it look like? *X4*
Is it **old**?
Yes, yes!
Is it gold?
Yes, yes, yes!
It's beautiful, it's old!
It's a bird, and it's **gold**!
Wow!

It's a bird!

Is it blue?

No! No!

What does it look like?

> I will learn words to describe things.

1 032 Listen, point, and repeat.

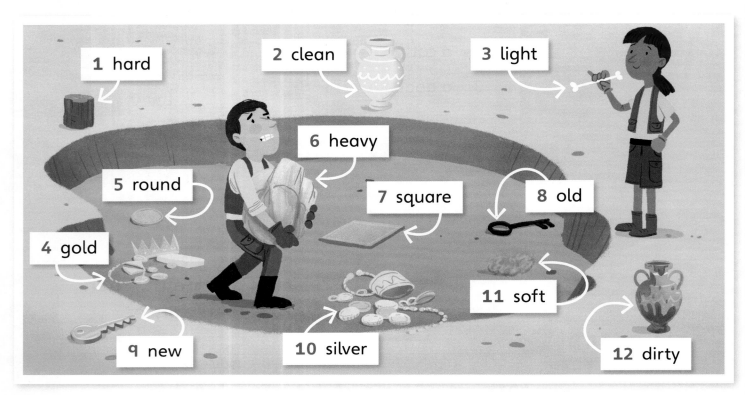

1 hard
2 clean
3 light
4 gold
5 round
6 heavy
7 square
8 old
9 new
10 silver
11 soft
12 dirty

2 033 What do the things in the picture look like? Listen and number.

3 Read and order the letters to make words.

(a) This teddy is   t f o s   _____ .

(b) This ball is   i d r y t   _____ .

(c) This pen is   l d o   _____ .

(d) This airplane is   e v h y a   _____ .

(e) This bowl is   l i v s r e   _____ .

4 Now talk to your partner.

It's soft.

The teddy!

Yes!

5 Count and write.

MATH ZONE

There are ...

a _____ silver things.

b _____ gold things.

c _____ square things.

d _____ round things.

e _____ hard things.

6 Listen and check ☑.

1 What does Debbie like?

a ☐   b ☐   c ☐

2 What is in the box?

a ☐   b ☐   c ☐

7 Make your own picture dictionary. Draw and label round and square things.

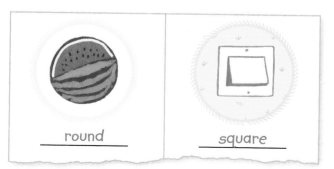

round   square

Language lab 1

GRAMMAR 1: MINE / YOURS / HIS / HERS

1 ▶ 035 **Watch. Whose hats are they? Write *Leo* or *Anna*.**

1 _____   2 _____

2 Choose 2 things each for you and your partner. Write mine or yours.

1 _____   2 _____

3 _____   4 _____

1 Whose is it? It's **mine**.
   My bag is old.

2 Whose is it? It's **yours**.
   Your bag is new.

3 Look at 2 again. Then choose.   my   mine   your   yours

1   The red coat is _____ .
    It's _____ coat.

2   The blue coat is _____ .
    It's _____ coat.

3   The green pencil case is _____ .
    It's _____ pencil case.

4   The yellow pencil case is _____ .
    It's _____ yellow pencil case.

4  **Play the *Whose is it?* game.**

> I have a yellow ruler. Whose is it?

> It's mine! It's my ruler!

1 This is Billy. His book is orange. It's **his**.

2 This is Rosa. Her book is purple. It's **hers**.

Values Help people in need.

5 **Read. Then circle and write his/her/hers.**

This is Mr. Smith.

oranges
bananas

This is **his** shopping list.

This is Mrs. Jones.

mangoes
apples

This is **her** shopping list.

Billy and Rosa help Mr. Smith and Mrs. Jones. They go to the store.

1 They are for Mr. Smith / Mrs. Jones . They are _____ mangoes. They are _____ .

2 They are for Mr. Smith / Mrs. Jones . They are _____ bananas. They are _____ .

3 They are for Mr. Smith / Mrs. Jones . They are _____ oranges. They are _____ .

6 **Work with a partner. Look at the fruit in 5 and say.**

> The oranges.

> They're his!

7 **How do you help other people? Talk in groups.**

Story lab

> I will read a story about something Anna finds.

1 🎧 036 💬 Read and listen. What does Anna find? Whose is it?

Cuckoo!

Tomato plants! Can you dig here please, Anna?

Yes, of course, Mr. Mud!

Mr. Mud, there is something hard here! What is it?

What does it look like?

It's square. It's dirty. It's made of wood.

There's a door! There's a bird! Whose is it?

It's my cuckoo clock! It's mine!

2 Look at the story. Check ☑ or cross ☒.

The cuckoo clock is …

1 clean ☐   2 dirty ☐

3 hard ☐   4 soft ☐

5 round ☐   6 square ☐

3 Look at the story. Then choose and write.

clock
wood
is
does

1 Whose _____ it?

2 It's my cuckoo _____ .

3 What _____ it look like?

4 It's made of _____ .

4 Mr. Mud has 4 keys. What do you think they open? Look at the key shapes. Then match.

a

b

c

d

1 car

2 house

3 box

4 clock

5 Act out the story in groups.

Phonics lab

U AND X

1 🎧 037 💬 Listen and repeat. Then write u or x.

1 b ___ g   2 n ___ t   3 r ___ n   4 si ___   5 ta ___ i

2 🎧 038 💬 Listen and chant.

Bugs in the **sun**!

A **bug** on the **rug**,

A **bug** in the **jug**,

Run, run, run away, **bugs**!

Run away, **run** away, **bugs**!

What's in the **box**?

There's a fox in the **box**!

There's an ox in the **box**!

There's a **fox** and an **ox** in the big, big **box**!

3 ✨ 💬 Make pattern cards. Then match and say the words.

CODE CRACKER

bug

taxi

nut

fox

4 🎧 039 💬 Listen and play the *Letter* game. Make "u" and "x" shapes!

Experiment lab
SCIENCE: SOLIDS AND LIQUIDS

I will learn about solids and liquids.

 Watch a video about solids and liquids.

EXPERIMENT TIME

How do some liquids change?

1 Make a non-Newtonian liquid.

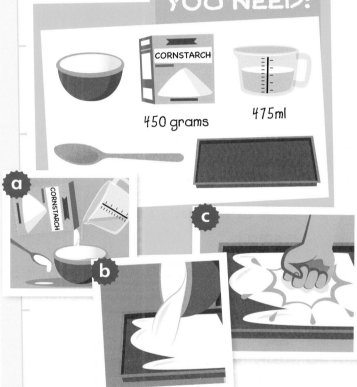

YOU NEED:

CORNSTARCH

450 grams

475ml

a

b

c

1  Listen and read.

waterfall

Water is a liquid. It has no shape. It isn't round or square. It isn't hard. It isn't soft.

rock

A rock is a solid. It has a shape. Solids have different shapes. This rock is round. Some solids are soft and some are hard. This rock is hard.

Liquids and solids can change.
This water isn't a liquid now. It's a solid.

2 Write **L** for liquid, **S** for solid.

1

2

2 What does your experiment tell you? Check ☑ or cross ☒.

1 I hit the liquid, and it is a liquid.

2 I hit the liquid, and it is a solid.

Language lab 2

GRAMMAR 2: OUR / OURS   THEIR / THEIRS

I will ask about objects using **ours** / **theirs**.

We have boxes of old toys!
Our box is yellow. **Ours** is yellow.
Their box is pink. **Theirs** is pink.

1 Choose and write.

Ours   Theirs   Our   Their

1   Look at the cars. Ours is red. _____ is black.

2   Their car is black. _____ car is red.

3   Look at the cats. Theirs is big. _____ is small.

4   Our cat is small. _____ cat is big.

2 Play the game in groups. Make a treasure chest. Put things in it.

3 Now ask and answer.

Our box is silver. What color is your box?

Ours is brown! There is a doll in ours!

A fun scavenger hunt!
COMMUNICATION

I will ask and answer about things and find them.

1 Listen and read. Who has to find the square clock?

This is my list, and this is yours. Let's find the things!

Find

a gold key

a round clock

a soft book

an old toy car

Find

a silver key

a square clock

a hard book

a new toy car

I can see a key! It's silver, not gold. It's yours. It's not mine!

2 Look at **1** and say, It's his/It's hers. What's the extra thing?

The square clock.

   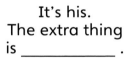

It's his. The extra thing is _____ .

3 Play the guessing game. Choose what you want to find and put them all in one box. Then guess with a partner.

old   new   liquid   solid   dirty   clean   soft   hard   red   green

Is it heavy?

Yes, it is! It's a ball!

4 Now count and complete the chart. Use the words in **3**.

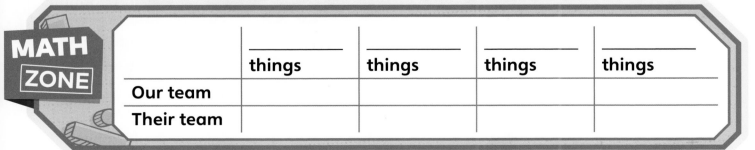

MATH ZONE	_____ things	_____ things	_____ things	_____ things
Our team				
Their team				

PROJECT AND REVIEW

Create a class museum

Step 1

Research

▷ What should we put in our museum?

- [ ] Think of a theme for the museum.
- [ ] Think about what you want to display.
- [ ] Think about groups of things.
- [ ] Choose a name.

Our Museum of Old Toys

Our Museum of Liquids and Solids

I have an idea! A museum of rocks!

Step 2

Plan

▷ What will our museum look like?

- [ ] Clear a space in the classroom.
- [ ] Think about how to make it look interesting.
- [ ] Collect the items.
- [ ] Decide how to arrange the items.

These marbles are solids!

We have marbles. They're hard and round.

They're beautiful!

The big things go here!

Step 3

Create

 How can we create our museum?

☐ Arrange the items.

☐ Make the labels.

This rock is old. It's from our schoolyard.

Step 4

Show and tell

 Show your museum to your friends. Talk about the items.

☐ Invite other classes to your museum.

 This is an owl. It's silver. It's mine!

Look at this car. It's new and gold.

💡 **Find out about museums in your country. Which one would you like to visit?**

This one! That one!

Now I can ...

... use words to describe things.

... talk about objects using **mine** / **yours** / **his** / **hers**.

... ask about objects using **ours** / **theirs**.

... ask and answer about things and find them.

1 Which painting do you like? Point and say.

2 Stick the frames on the happy, sad, and angry paintings.

3 Order the pictures. Write 1–4.

CODE CRACKER

A

B

C

D

4 Listen and point. Then sing along and dance.

SONG TIME

My friends

He's never **angry**,
He's sometimes **shy**.
He's always **kind** and **happy**.
He's my friend, he's my friend!

She's never angry.
She's sometimes shy.
She's always kind and happy.
She's my friend, she's my friend!

angry!

shy!

happy!

I am happy!

VOCABULARY

> *I will learn describing words for people and pets.*

1 🎧 043 💬 Listen, point, and repeat.

1 angry

2 happy

3 sad

4 funny

5 kind

6 friendly

7 shy

8 helpful

9 naughty

10 lazy

11 young

12 tired

2 💡 Who am I? Read 3 clues. Then circle a or b.

1 I'm happy.
I'm helpful.
I'm not old.

2 I'm sad.
I'm lazy.
I'm not funny.

3 I'm funny.
I'm friendly.
I'm not young.

4 I'm shy.
I'm young.
I'm not angry.

3 Now say three clues about the pictures for your partner to guess.

4 Label the people and pets. Use all the words from **1**.

1 _____ 2 _____ 3 _____ 4 _____

5 _____ 6 _____ 7 _____ 8 _____

9 _____ 10 _____ 11 _____ 12 _____

5 Now point at **4** and say.

I like this man. He is funny!

6 Make headbands and play the *Mime* game.

Am I shy?

I'm Sad

Am I sad?

No, you aren't.

Yes, you are!

7 Make your own picture dictionary. Draw happy, sad, and funny faces and write.

_____ happy _____   _____ sad _____

Language lab 1

GRAMMAR 1: HE / SHE   IS / ISN'T

I will describe people using **always / sometimes / never**.

1  **Watch. Circle the correct word.**

Leo is sad / shy / angry .

Is he sad?

No, **he isn't**.

He's happy.

2 **What do you think? Look, choose, and write.**

She/He is …   She/He isn't …   Yes, she/he is.   No, she/he isn't.

1

2

3

Is she happy?

_____

_____ friendly.

_____ sad.

Is he tired? _____

_____ young.

_____ angry.

Is she shy? _____

_____ old.

_____ friendly.

3 **Talk about your ideas. Work with a partner.**

Look at Picture 1 … she's happy.

Is she happy, or is she sad?

He is **always** happy.　　　She is **sometimes** happy.　　　He is **never** happy.

4 **Listen and circle.**

friendly: always / sometimes / never　　　naughty: always / sometimes / never

5 **Ask your partner. Then check ☑ or cross ☒ .**

	always	sometimes	never
friendly			
naughty			
helpful			
lazy			
shy			
happy			

Are you lazy?

No, I'm never lazy.

Oh, I'm sometimes lazy!

6 **Look at 5. Write your partner's answers.**

He's/She's　always/sometimes/never

1 _____ lazy.

2 _____ naughty.

3 _____ helpful.

4 _____ friendly.

5 _____ shy.

6 _____ happy.

7 **Play Who is it? in groups.**

She's sometimes shy.
She's never lazy.

Is it Amy?

Yes, it is!

Story lab

READING

I will read a story about a painting competition.

1 🔧 046 💬 **Read and listen. Who wins the gold cup?**

Who is this?

- I have my paints.
- Great! I have pencils and crayons.
- I have a photo!

2 Who is this, Tom?

It's my cousin. He's sometimes naughty and always happy!

3

- Who is this, Mrs. Hay?
- It's my friend.
- Is she angry? She looks angry.
- Er ... no ... she's sad.

4 This is very good, Mr. Mud!

Thank you. Milly is sometimes naughty, but she is friendly.

2 Look at the story. Then read, choose, and write.

    rainbow   friend   cousin   Milly

1   Tom paints his _____ .

2   Mrs. Hay paints her _____ .

3   Mr. Mud paints _____ .

4   Milly paints a _____ .

5
OK, finish your pictures now, please!

6
The gold cup goes to … Mr. Mud!

Congratulations, Mr. Mud!

7
Look at Milly!

8
It's a rainbow! Milly, you are very funny!

3 Look at the story again. What are they like? Match and say.

1

2

3

- a She's sad.

- b She's sometimes naughty, but she is friendly.

- c He's sometimes naughty and always happy.

Is Tom's cousin sad?

No, he isn't. He's always happy!

4 Look at the story again. Then number the sentences in order.

a The gold cup goes to … Mr. Mud!

b Who is this, Mrs. Hays?

c Look at Milly!

d Is she angry? She looks angry.

e It's a rainbow! Milly, you are very funny!

5 Act out the story in groups.

Phonics lab

> I will learn the **j** and **y** sounds.

1 🎧 047 Listen and repeat. Then write j or y.

1 ___eans

2 ___uice

3 ___ar

4 ___oung

5 ___ogurt

6 ___ak

2 🎧 048 💬 Listen and chant.

Is it **your yellow yo-yo**, is it **yours**?

Is it **your yellow yo-yo**, is it **yours**?

Yes, yes, yes!

Jump in the **jungle**,

Jump, jump, jump!

Jump like a **jaguar**,

Jump, jump, jump!

3 🎧 049 💬 Listen and play the game.

J = arms up   Y = arms crossed

4 Make invisible words. Write with lemon juice.

Experiment lab

ART AND DESIGN: CHANGING FACES

> *I will learn about changing faces.*

 Watch a video about faces.

EXPERIMENT TIME

1 🔊 **Listen and read. Then circle.**

We have **muscles** in our faces. The muscles move our mouths, eyes, noses, and eyebrows.

muscles

Sometimes our eyes look big, and sometimes they look small. Sometimes our mouths look small, and sometimes they are big and open.

Artists paint and draw the muscles in a face. They use colors and lines and different shapes.

1 😊   **2** 😐   I can see muscles in picture 1 / 2 .

2 Match. There is one extra sentence.

He looks angry.   He is tired.

He looks sad.   He is happy.

How do you change?

1 💬 **Work with a partner. One person laughs, yawns, or cries. What happens to you?**

My partner	Me
laughs 	I laugh . / I don't laugh .
yawns 	I yawn . / I don't yawn .
cries 	I cry . / I don't cry .

2 Now circle for you.

I always / sometimes / never do the same as my partner.

Language lab 2

GRAMMAR 2: DO YOU HAVE ...?

1 Complete the questions. Then answer Yes, I do or No, I don't.

have
you
Do

> **Do you have** a brother?
> Yes, I do. He's funny!
>
> **Do you have** a sister?
> No, I don't.

1 _____ you have a cousin?
   _____

2 Do you _____ a bird? _____

3 Do _____ have a red hat? _____

4 _____ _____ _____ a blue pencil case? _____

2 Play *Tic Tac Toe* with a partner.

Yes, I do = ☑   No, I don't = ☒

cat	rabbit	red bag
green eraser	brother	silver ruler
white teddy	blue coat	sister

> Do you have a red bag?

> No, I don't.

It's a rabbit.

Its fur is white.

3 🔊 051 Listen and read. Then circle and write.

> Do you have a cat?

> Yes, I do. It's orange. Its fur is soft.

It's   Its

1 Do you have a dog?
   Yes, I do. _____
   black / white .
   _____ tail is
   brown / black .

2 Do you have a rabbit?
   Yes, I do. _____
   white / gray .
   _____ nose is
   blue / pink .

Let's take a photo!
COMMUNICATION

I will talk about funny photos.

1 Listen and read.

1 This is my new phone. Its camera is really good.

Let's take a photo.

Yes, a selfie!

2 Okay ... now ... wait.

3 Oh, that's a funny photo!

2 Choose a funny photo. Work with a partner. Ask and answer.

Do you have orange hair?

No, I don't.

Are you sad?

Yes, I am.

Number 1!

Values Ask people before you take photos.

3 Who wants a photo? Check ☑ or cross ☒. Then listen and check.

Let's take a photo.

4 Read. Then circle for you.

I take photos of my friends.
I ask / don't ask my friends.

PROJECT AND REVIEW

Create a portrait gallery

Step 1

Research

 Who shall I paint?

- [ ] Think about what questions to ask them.
- [ ] Collect some paintings and photos for ideas.

Who to paint?

My friend?	Mom?
My cousin?	Me?
Our teacher?	

Step 2

Plan

 What do we need to do and ask?

- [ ] Interview the people we are painting.
- [ ] Get paints, paper, glue, pencils, and crayons.
- [ ] Choose a style of painting.
- [ ] Decide where to display the pictures.

- What's your name?
- Are you always happy?
- Do you have a pet?
- What's your favorite color?

Step 3

Create

> How do we create our portrait gallery?

- [ ] Draw, paint, or take photos.
- [ ] Write about the people.
- [ ] Put the work on a wall.

Step 4

Show and tell

> Talk about the people and the paintings.

Who's this?

It's our teacher! She's always kind.

She looks happy! It's a great painting!

Here, she looks funny and friendly.

Talk about old and new photos.

Look!

Now I can ...

... use describing words.

... describe people using **always** / **sometimes** / **never**.

... ask and answer about people and objects using **have**.

... talk about funny photos.

1 🎧 054 Listen and follow. Say the number.

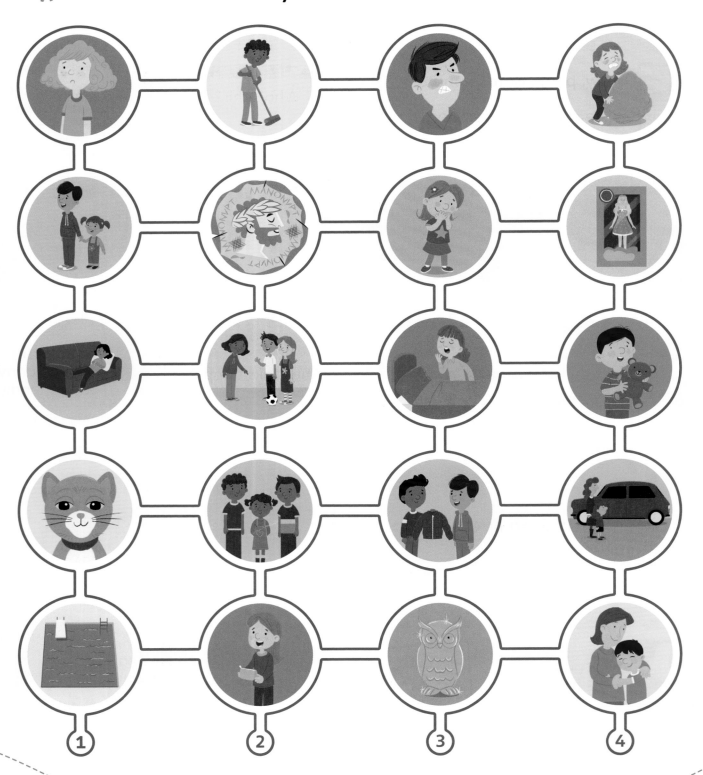

2 Read and follow. Draw the arrows. ← → ↑ ↓

1
Do you have a sister?
Yes, I do. ◯

Is she happy? No, she isn't.
She's sad. ◯

He's helpful! ◯

It's round. ◯

She's sometimes shy.

2
Is it heavy? Yes, it is! ◯

This doll is new. ◯

It's my teddy! It's mine! ◯

She's tired. ◯

Whose is it? Is it your coat?

3 Follow the arrows. Choose and write.

round   have   angry   Is   He's

kind   ours   your   tired   mine

1
_____ she lazy? Yes, she is! ↑

Do you _____ a sister?
Yes, I do. →

It's _____ . ↑

_____ helpful. →

He's _____ !

2
My mom is _____ . ↑

This is our car. It's _____ . ←

Whose is it? Is it _____ coat? ↑

She's _____ . →

This teddy is _____ .

4 💬 Ask and answer with a partner.

What's this?

It's a silver owl.

Music around the world

1 Look at the pictures. What instruments can you see? Say.

2 (055) Listen and read.

Drums

sticks

You bang drums.

These girls and boys are from Japan. They play drums. Their drums are round and hard. They are made from wood. The drums are heavy!

Fun Fact!

Some drums are as big as cars!

Bagpipes

pipes

bag

You blow bagpipes.

This boy is from Scotland. He plays the bagpipes. He is called a piper.

Bagpipes have a soft bag and long pipes.

Veenas

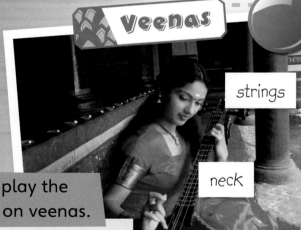

strings

neck

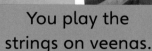

You play the strings on veenas.

This woman is from India. She plays a veena. Veenas are big and round. They have a long neck. They have strings. Very good music comes from light veenas, not heavy veenas.

3 🎵 056 **What is it? Listen to the music and check ☑ .**

It's a ...	veena	bagpipe	drum
1			
2			
3			

4 🎵 057 **Listen again. How does the music make you feel? Choose and write.**

> happy   sad   angry   tired   good   bad   lazy

1   I feel _____ .   2   I feel _____ .   3   I feel _____ .

5 💬 **Now tell a partner.**   > It's happy music! I feel good!

My Culture

Find out about traditional instruments in your country.

6 ⚙️ **Make a string instrument.**

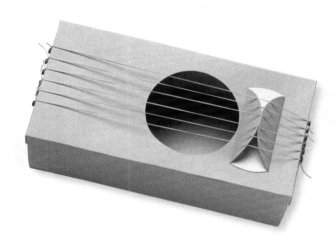

1   Take a tissue box. Fold and stick card on the box.

2   Stick pins in the box.

3   Put the rubber bands around the pins.

4   Play your instrument!

> It has strings. It's not heavy.

7 💬 **Describe your instrument.**

5 Come in!

How can I create a class meal?

1 💬 **What do you like in this house? Point and say.**

2 💡 **Stick the food on the table. Then draw lines to match.**

3 What do you say? Circle.

1 Thank you! / Come in!

2 Thank you! / Hello!

3 Goodbye! / Come in!

4 058 Listen and point. Then sing along and dance.

Come in!

SONG TIME

Make yourself at home!

Come in and make yourself
at home,
We're happy that you're here,
Come in and make yourself
at home,
It's great to have you here.

Would you like some **pasta**?
Would you like some **cheese**?
Would you like some **cookies**?

Yes, please!

Repeat chorus

Would you like ...?

Do you like cookies?

VOCABULARY

I will learn food words.

1 059 Listen, point, and repeat.

1 chicken   2 cheese   3 bread   4 rice

5 soup   6 salad   7 cookies   8 water

9 juice   10 ice cream   11 pasta   12 fish

2 You have $20. What would you like in the café? Decide and write.

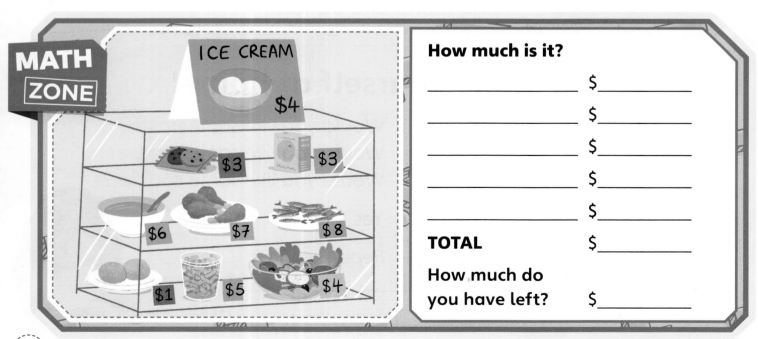

MATH ZONE

ICE CREAM $4

$3 $3

$6 $7 $8

$1 $5 $4

How much is it?

_____ $_____

_____ $_____

_____ $_____

_____ $_____

_____ $_____

TOTAL $_____

How much do you have left? $_____

3 Look, match and write the food.

 1

 2

 3

a Café menu

_____

_____

_____

_____

b Grocery list

_____

_____

_____

_____

c Make a sandwich!

_____

_____

_____

_____

4 Look at 3. Then ask and answer.

She has fish and soup.

3 a !

Yes!

Do you like fish?

Yes, I do. I don't like soup!

5 Now ask and answer with a partner.

I have soup.

How much is it?

It's six dollars. And you?

I have cookies and water.

6 Make your own picture dictionary. Draw or write your favorite food words.

ice cream

salad

Language lab 1

GRAMMAR 1: CAN I HAVE ...?

1 ▷ 🎧060 **Watch. What does Leo ask for?**
Check ☑ or cross ☒ .

| fish | ☐ | rice | ☐ | bread | ☐ | apples | ☐ |
| oranges | ☐ | chicken | ☐ | pasta | ☐ | bananas | ☐ |

2 🎧060 **Watch again. Then choose and write.**

Milly   Leo and his friends
Mrs. Hay

The food is for _____ .

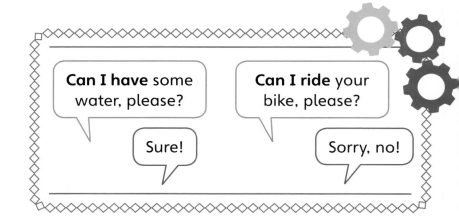

Can I have some water, please?

Can I ride your bike, please?

Sure!

Sorry, no!

3 **What do they need? Look, choose, and write.**

bread   pasta   cheese   rice

1   Can I have some _____ , please?

2   Can I have _____ , please?

3   Can I _____ ?

4   _____

4 Order and write to find out what they need. Then match a–e.

pencil   a   have   I

1 Can _____ , please? ☐

I   please   water   some   have   Can

2 _____ , _____ ? ☐

have   I   Can   a   please   bag

3 _____ , _____ ? ☐

an   Can   please   I   have   eraser

4 _____ , _____ ? ☐

some   have   please   can   cookies   we

5 _____ , _____ ? ☐

a

b

c   1+1 = 3

d $ 9.00

e

5 Play the game. Ask and answer.

Can I have two apples, please?

Sorry, no!

Can I have one apple?

Sure!

Story lab

> I will read a story about Tom's cousin.

1 🔧 061 💬 Read and listen. Who comes to Tom's house?

Come over and play!

1 It's nine o'clock! School! I'm late!

Tom, it's Saturday. No school today!

Hooray!

2 Can I play with my toys, Mom?

Yes, sure!

3 Tom, look! Grandma and Aunt Julia are here! And your cousin, Adam!

Come in!

Hello, Tom!

4 Can I have some water, please?

Can I have some juice, please?

Yes, of course!

2 Circle T (True) or F (False).

1 This is my grandma. T / F
2 This is my aunt. T / F
3 This is my mom. T / F
4 This is my cousin. T / F

3 Complete and match.

1 Can I _____ with my toys, Mom? ●

2 Can I have _____ water, please? ●

3 Can I _____ this book? ●

● a Okay.

● b Yes, sure!

● c Yes, of course!

4 Look and think. What toys does Adam play with? Check ☑ or cross ☒.

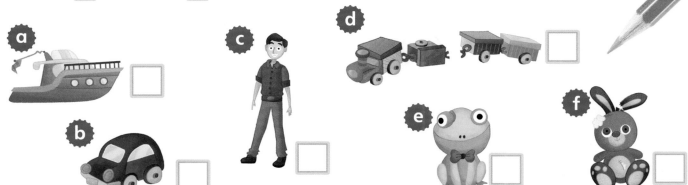

5 Act out the story in groups.

Phonics lab

CH AND SH

1 🎧 062 Listen and repeat. Then write ch or sh.

1 ___air   2 ___ips   3 ___ess

4 ___ip   5 ___elf   6 ___op

2 🎧 063 💬 Listen and chant.

Chicken and **cherries**, **chips** and **cheese**!

Yes, please!

Chicken and **cherries**, **chips** and **cheese**!

A **shirt** in the **shop**.

Shoes in the **shop**.

Shorts in the **shop**.

And a **sheep** in the **shop**!

3 🎧 064 💬 Listen and play the game.

ch = dance   sh = stop!

4 💬 Make shapes and play with a partner.

Sh sh sh

Yes!

Is it a shirt?

sheep   **sh**

Experiment lab
TECHNOLOGY: MILK

I will learn about making milk.

 ▶ **Watch a video about milk.**

1 **065 Listen, read, and match. Write a–d.**

We get milk from animals: cows, sheep, goats, and horses **1** ☐ . We also get milk from plants like coconuts, almonds, and soya beans **2** ☐ .

Farmers pick the nuts and beans from trees and plants. They sometimes use combine harvesters to help them **3** ☐ . The nuts and beans go to factories **4** ☐ . Machines get the milk from the plants and make it clean and healthy.

2 💬 **Talk with a partner.**

> Do you drink milk from goats?

> Yes, I do!

EXPERIMENT TIME

Can you make ice cream?

You can use plant or animal milk!

salt
ice

1 Milk, sugar, and vanilla

2 Ice and salt

The salt makes the ice extra cold!

5 minutes!

3 Close the bags!

4 Shake, shake, shake!

Open the small bag.

Do you have ice cream?
Yes / No

Language lab 2
GRAMMAR 2: CAN I HAVE THIS / THAT ...?

I will ask and answer about objects using this / that.

1 **Choose and complete. Write this or that ...**

1 Can I have _____ _____ , please?

2 Can I have _____ _____ , please?

3 Can I have _____ _____ , please?

2 **Read and check ☑ .**

1

Can I have an ice cream, please?

This one or that one?

That one!

2

Can I have a salad, please?

This one or that one?

This one!

3

Can I have a juice, please?

This one or that one?

This one!

Can I have this salad, please?

Can I have that salad, please?

3  **Play This or That.**

Can I have a book, please?

Sure! This one or that one?

This one! No ... that one!

Let's order some food!

COMMUNICATION

I will ask and answer about food.

1 Complete the conversations. Then read them with a partner.

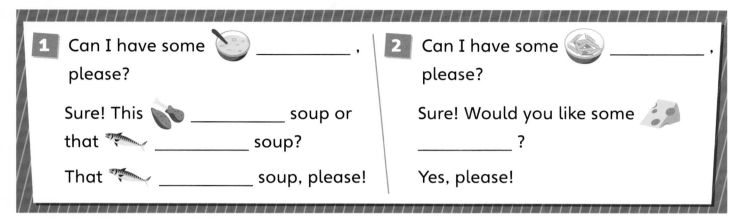

1 Can I have some _____ , please?

Sure! This _____ soup or that _____ soup?

That _____ soup, please!

2 Can I have some _____ , please?

Sure! Would you like some _____ ?

Yes, please!

2 Read and circle the incorrect word. Then write the correct word and say with a partner.

1

Can I have chicken and rice, please?

Sure. Here you go.

Thank you.

_____

2

Can I have some bread, soup, and water, please?

Yes. Here you go.

Thanks.

_____

Values Be kind. Ask people what they like and don't like.

3 Work with a partner. Ask, answer, and draw.

Would you like chicken today?

No, thank you. Can I have some pasta, please!

Sure!

4 Do you know what food your friends like and don't like? Say.

PROJECT AND REVIEW

Create a class meal

Step 1

Research

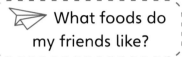 What foods do I need?

- [ ] Write a food survey.
- [ ] Ask and answer.
- [ ] Record the answers.

Do you like:

chicken? [ ]

rice? [ ]

salad? [ ]

Step 2

Plan

What foods do my friends like?

- [ ] Look at your results.
- [ ] Choose foods that a lot of people like.
- [ ] What foods are good together?
- [ ] Plan a meal.

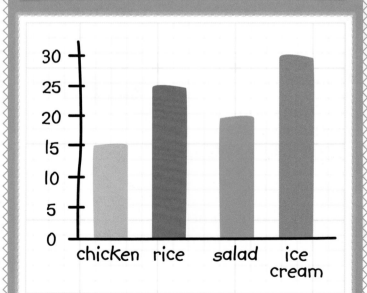

Step 3

Create

 How can I make my meal?

- ☐ Look at your plan.
- ☐ Draw or stick the food on paper plates.
- ☐ Design and make a menu.

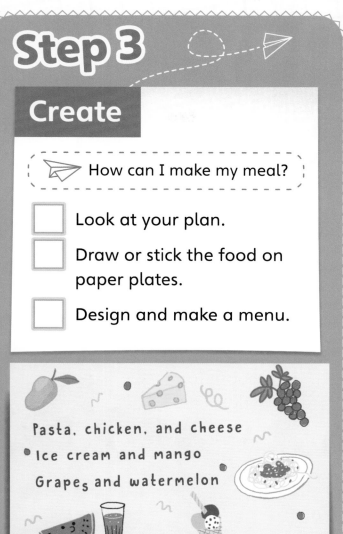

Pasta, chicken, and cheese
• Ice cream and mango
Grapes and watermelon

Step 4

Show and tell

Role-play a restaurant scene.

Student A

Ask for your favorite food.

Student B

You are a waiter. Do you have that food?

Can I have some pasta, chicken, and cheese?

Sure! Here you go!

Have a picnic with your friends.

I like bread and cheese and apples!

Me, too!

Now I can ...

- ... use food words.
- ... ask for things politely using **Can I have ...?**
- ... ask and answer about objects using **this / that**.
- ... ask and answer about food.

6 Sports Day

How can I organize a sports day?

1 What sports do you like? Point and say.

2 Stick the items on the picture.

3 Order the pictures. Write 1–4.

CODE CRACKER

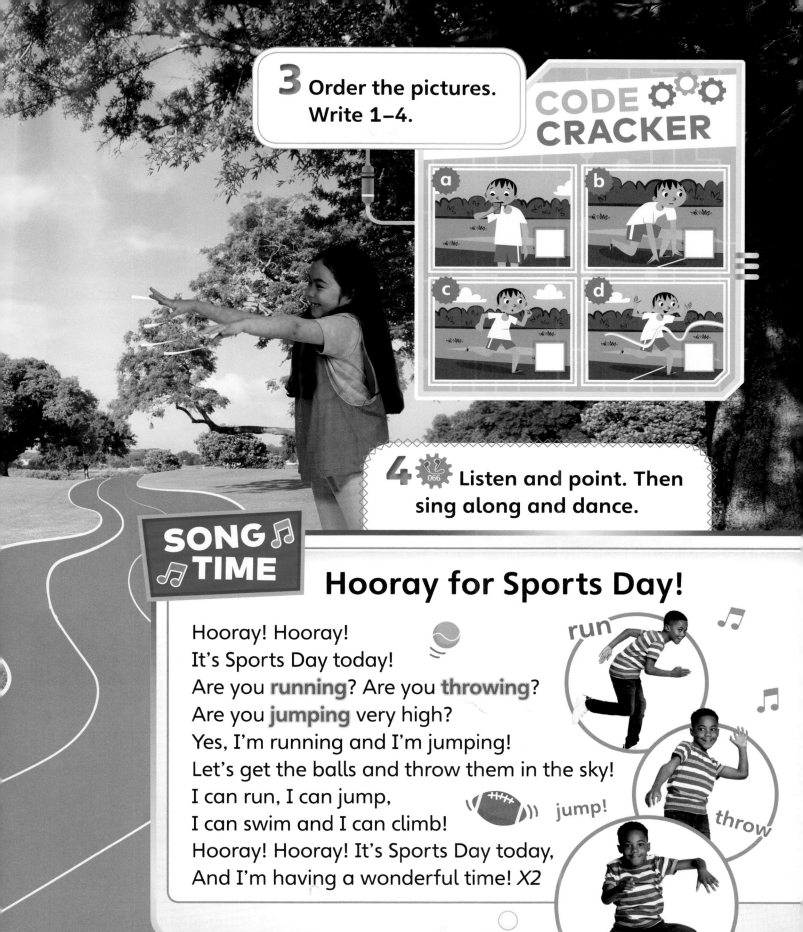

4 🎧 066 Listen and point. Then sing along and dance.

SONG TIME

Hooray for Sports Day!

Hooray! Hooray!
It's Sports Day today!
Are you **running**? Are you **throwing**?
Are you **jumping** very high?
Yes, I'm running and I'm jumping!
Let's get the balls and throw them in the sky!
I can run, I can jump,
I can swim and I can climb!
Hooray! Hooray! It's Sports Day today,
And I'm having a wonderful time! *X2*

run

jump!

throw

Do you play soccer?
VOCABULARY

I will learn sport and activity words.

1 Listen, point, and repeat. 067

 1 table tennis

 2 volleyball

 3 soccer

 4 basketball

 5 team

 6 kick

 7 throw

 8 catch

 9 watch

 10 hit

 11 jump

 12 run

2 Match and write.

 1 _____

 2 _____

 3 _____

 4 _____

 a

 b

 c

 d

3 Ask and answer with a partner.

Do you play volleyball?

Yes! And basketball. What about you?

4 Look at pictures 1–7 and write. Use words from 1. Then write the words for each sport.

1

2

3

4

_____

_____

_____

_____

5

6

7

_____

_____

_____

basketball	volleyball	table tennis	soccer

5 Work with a partner. Ask and answer.

Do you run in soccer?

Yes, you do!

Do you kick in table tennis?

No, you don't!

6 Make your own picture dictionary. Add your favorite sport words.

kick

table tennis

Language lab 1

I will talk about actions using **I'm ...ing**.

1 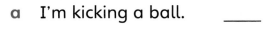 Watch. Then write Anna or Leo.

1 I'm throwing. _____

2 I'm watching. _____

I'm jumping
= I am jumping.
You're jumping
= You are jumping.
Are you swimming?
No, I'm not.
Are you jumping?
Yes, I am.

2 Who is it? Look, match, and write 1–6.

reading   swimming   climbing   kicking   running   throwing

a I'm kicking a ball. ____

b I'm swimming. ____

c I'm running. ____

d I'm throwing. ____

e I'm reading. ____

f I'm climbing. ____

3 🎧 Listen and check ☑ a, b, or c.

1

a ☐   b ☐   c ☐

2

a ☐   b ☐   c ☐

4 💬 Write. Then check ☑ the activities you like. Act them out. Say I'm …

1 I'm _____   2 _____   3 _____   4 _____

5 ⚙️ 💬 Make a sports person. Then play a guessing game.

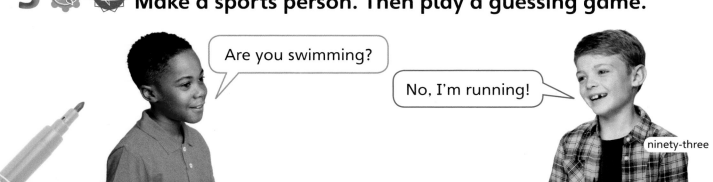

Are you swimming?

No, I'm running!

Story lab

READING

I will read a story about a game of soccer.

1  **Read and listen. What are the two teams called?**

GOAL!

1 Good luck, Castle School!

Look at Milly! She likes soccer!

2 Run, Anna! Are you running, Leo?

I'm running!

I'm not running. I'm jumping!

3 Goal!

Great goal, Leo!

4 Goal!

The score is River School 1, Castle School 1.

2 **Who says it? Choose and write.**

Miss Kelly Tom Leo Anna

1 I'm running! _____

2 I'm not running! _____

3 I'm jumping! _____

4 I'm kicking! _____

5 I'm coming! _____

6 You're playing soccer! _____

5 Kick, Leo!

I'm kicking!

6 Ow! My leg!

I'm coming, Leo!

7 Goal!

Great goal, Milly! You're playing soccer!

8 River School 1, Castle School 1, and Milly 1!

3 Read. How many goals in total?

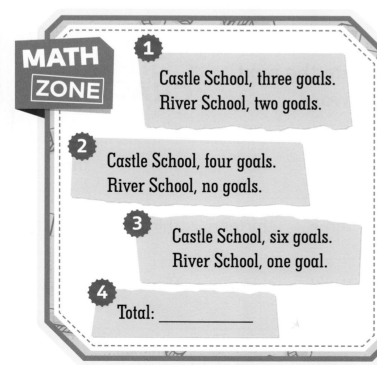

MATH ZONE

1 Castle School, three goals.
River School, two goals.

2 Castle School, four goals.
River School, no goals.

3 Castle School, six goals.
River School, one goal.

4 Total: _____

4 Circle. Then listen and check.

River school are 1 yellow / red , and Castle School are 2 green / blue !

Yes! Goal!

Castle School 3 1 / 2 , River School 0!

Oh, now a goal for River School!

4 River / My School 1, Castle School 1.

5 Act out the story in groups.

I will learn the **th** sounds.

1 072 Listen and repeat. Then write th.

1 ___at 2 ___ese 3 ___ere 4 ___ank 5 ___irteen 6 ___row

2 073 Listen and chant.

They have **this** and **that**, **this** and **that**.

They have **these** and **those**, **these** and **those**!

Throw three things!
Throw three things!
Three things,
three things,
Throw three things!

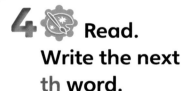

3 074 Listen and play the game.

this, that, these, those

thank, three, thirteen, throw

4 Read. Write the next th word.

CODE CRACKER

1	this	that	this	that
	_____			
2	three	thirteen	thirteen	three
	_____			
3	thank	thing	throw	thank
	_____			

Experiment lab
MATH: MEASURING

I will learn about measuring things in sports.

 Watch a video about measuring.

1  Listen and read.

In many sports, we measure things. We measure how far we can jump or run or swim. We measure how high we can jump. We measure how high a table tennis net is. We measure how big a soccer field is. We measure how big a basketball court is.

We can measure the air in our lungs, too!

lungs

2 Look and circle.

I'm (jumping / measuring).
How far you can jump? Say.

3 Read and write the answer.

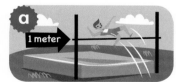
a 1 meter

b 30 meters

1   How far can she swim?

   She can swim _____ meters.

2   How high can he jump?

   He can jump _____ meter.

EXPERIMENT TIME

How much air is in your lungs? How far can you blow?

1 Blow and measure.

One blow!

How big is your balloon?

_____ centimeters?

2 Circle for you.

There is (a lot of / a little) air in my lungs.

3 Find and measure the objects. Then complete the chart.

	How many centimeters?
(pencil)	
(crumpled paper)	
(straw)	

I will ask and answer about actions using **Can you ...?**

1 Choose and write. Then check ☑ the correct answer.

swim   Can   you

Can you ride a bike?

Yes, **I can.**   No, **I can't.**

1   Can you _____ ?   Yes, I can. ☐   No, I can't. ☐

2   _____ you climb this wall?   Yes, I can. ☐   No, I can't. ☐

3   Can _____ kick?   Yes, I can. ☐   No, I can't. ☐

2 Can you do it? Try. Then write Yes, I can or No, I can't.

Can you draw an octopus?

_____

Can you dance and say: "A fox in a box."?

_____

Can you throw and catch two balls?

_____

Can you jump and sing?

_____

3 Make a throwing game. Then play with a partner.

Can you do this?

No. Can you?

Yes!

Well done!

Can you juggle?
COMMUNICATION

> I will talk about activities with my friends.

1 🎧 076 Listen and read. Circle the correct word.

1
Can you juggle?

What does juggle / jump mean?

2
You throw and catch / kick two balls. Can you juggling / juggle?

Yes / No, I can't!

3
I can help you! Watch me! Are you juggle / juggling?

Yes, I am! I'm juggling! Thank you!

2 💬 Learn to juggle. Then say.

JUGGLE WITH TWO HATS!

I'm throwing!

Now I'm catching!

Now juggle with balls!

Values I share my skills and help my friends to do things.

3 💬 Ask and answer with a partner. Write yes or no.

Can you do this?

	Me	My partner	We can help each other.
Yoga!			
Hula hoop!			

4 💬 What new skills can you teach a friend? Say.

PROJECT AND REVIEW

Organize a Sports Day

Step 1

Research

 What will our Sports Day include?

- [ ] Ask classmates what games and sports they can play.
- [ ] Choose our favorites.

	Table tennis	Hula hoop	Balloon volleyball
Sofia	✓	✓	✓
Darios	✓	✗	✓
Chen	✗	✓	✓

Can you play balloon volleyball?

No!

I can help you.

Thanks!

Step 2

Plan

 What do we need to do?

- [ ] Choose a place to do the activities.
- [ ] Make a list of things we need.
- [ ] Decide what we need to make.

We have	We don't have
balls	balloons

Step 3

Create

 How can we organize our Sports Day?

☐ Prepare the space for your day.

☐ Create your games.

☐ Draw and write a program.

Our Sports Day

Balloon volleyball

Sack race

Table tennis

Watch your friends play sports and cheer them on. +

Great game!

Step 4

Show and tell

 Play the games and sports.

☐ Help each other.

I'm in the sack race.

Are you running in the sack?

No. You can't run in a sack. I'm jumping.

Now I can ...

... use sport and activity words.

... talk about actions using **I'm ...ing.**

... ask and answer about actions using **Can you ...?**

... talk about activities with my friends.

3 Checkpoint

UNITS 5 AND 6

1 Listen and follow. Say the number.

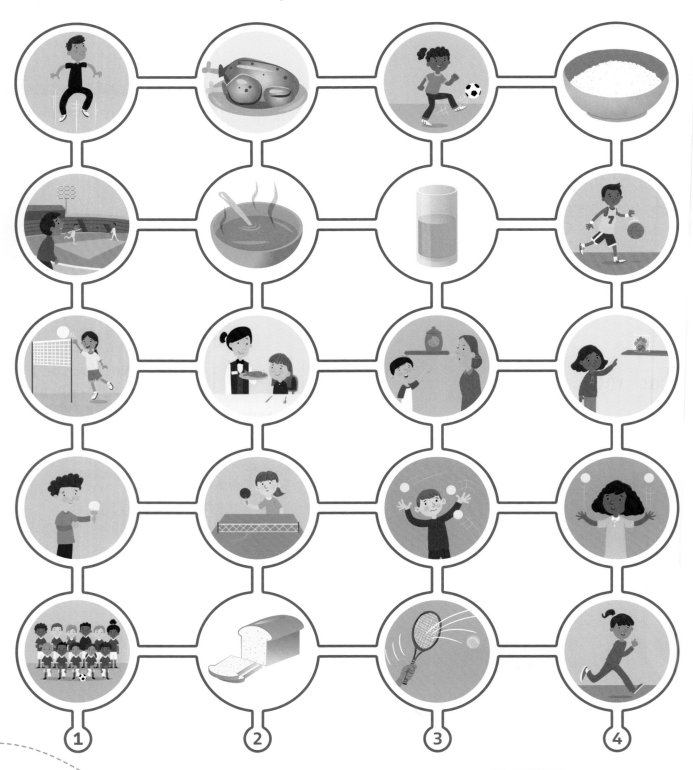

2 Read and follow. Draw the arrows. ← → ↑ ↓

1
Are you playing volleyball?
Yes, I am. ◯

Would you like some fish?
Yes, please. ◯

Can I have some soup, please? ◯

Can I have some juice, please? ◯

Can you kick? Yes, I can!

2
Can I have some chicken, please? ◯

Are you jumping? Yes, I am! ◯

I'm watching a game. I'm not playing. ◯

Are you playing volleyball? Yes, I am. ◯

3 Follow the arrows. Choose and write.

Can   I'm   juice   cookies   that

rice   chicken   have   basketball   Yes

1
_____ running. ↑

_____ you throw two balls? Yes, I can! ↑

Can I have _____ salad, please? ←

Can I have some _____ , please? Sorry, no. ↑

Can I have some _____ , please?

2
Can I _____ some soup, please? ↑

Can I have some _____ , please? →

Can you kick? _____ , I can! →

Can I have some _____ , please? ↓

I'm playing _____ .

4 Ask and answer with a partner.

Can you kick?

Yes, I can.

Amazing boat races

CULTURE

1 💬 **Look at the pictures. What do you think they are doing?**

2 📞 **Listen and read.**

> I'm watching boats on a river. It's a boat race!

> Zongzi is my favorite food!

Dragon boats

It is the Dragon Boat Festival in Yueyang, in China. The Dragon Boat festival is in June.

There are lots of teams in boats. The boats are beautiful colors. There are dragon heads on the boats.

You sit down in the dragon boats. There are drums on the boats, too. This man is hitting a drum.

There is special food for the festival. Zongzi is made with rice. There are leaves around the rice.

Gondolas

> This famous food from Venice is called rise e bise in Italian. It's delicious!

These boats are called gondolas. They are in Venice, in Italy. Every year, in September, there is a gondola race. The boats are very beautiful. They are red and yellow and silver and gold. You stand up in the gondolas.

Fun Fact!

The winners of the gondola race get red flags!

3 Read and circle the correct answer.

1   The Dragon Boat race is in Italy / China .

2   The gondola race is in Italy / China .

3   There is a drum on the Dragon Boats / gondolas .

4   You stand up in Dragon Boats / gondolas .

5   They win flags in the Dragon Boat race / Gondola race .

6   Zongzi is made with rice and leaves / rice and peas .

4 Imagine you are at the boat races. Ask and answer.

> I'm watching dragon boats.

> You're in China!

My Culture

Find out about traditional or famous boat races in your country.

5 Make a Dragon Boat.

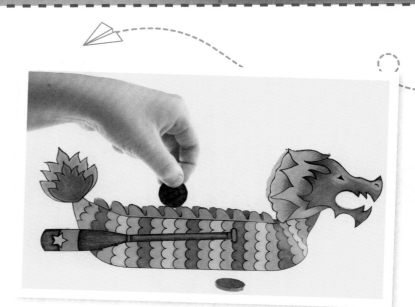

1   Cut out some card.

2   Draw some lines.

3   Fold the card.

4   Use sticky tape.

5   Stick the coins.

6   Make a dragon head and tail. Your boat is ready!

> This is my dragon boat. This is the dragon head!

6 Describe your boat to your partner.

7 Our home!

How can I design a dream house?

1 💬 **What is your favorite place in this house? Point and say.**

This is my favorite place. It's great!

2 ⚙️ **Stick the items in the rooms.**

1 I'm sleeping.

2 I'm making a salad.

3 I'm brushing my teeth.

3 Look at the drawing. Check the correct sentence.

CODE CRACKER

I'm drawing a house.

1   I'm drawing one big square, four small squares, a triangle, and a rectangle. ☐

2   I'm drawing five big squares, one small triangle, and two rectangles. ☐

4 🎧 079 Listen and point. Then sing along and dance.

SONG TIME 🎵

Beautiful house

This is our house,
It's a beautiful house!
It has everything that we need.
A **bedroom**, a **bathroom**, a **kitchen**
And space to play and read!

This is our house,
It's a beautiful house!
It has everything that we like.
A bedroom, a bathroom, a kitchen
And space to ride a bike!

zzz

wash hands

make a cake

What's in the bedroom?
VOCABULARY

1 🎧 080 Listen, point, and repeat.

 1 bedroom

 2 bathroom

 3 living room

 4 kitchen

 5 yard

 6 cook

 7 look for

 8 clean

 9 take a shower

 10 make a cake

 11 drink

 12 do homework

2 🎧 081 Listen and circle T (True) or F (False).

1 There's a lizard in the bedroom!   T / F

2 There's a fox in the bathroom!   T / F

3 There's an owl in the kitchen!   T / F

4 There's a bat in the living room!   T / F

3 💬 Now say all the sentences correctly.

There's a lizard in the kitchen!

4 **What's on Lisa's "to do" list?**
   Look at the pictures and match.

a   I look for my shoes.   ☐

b   I take a shower.   ☐

c   I clean my bedroom.   ☐

d   I drink some juice.   ☐

5 **What's on your "to do" list? Look
   and write. Use all the words in 1.**

To do …

 _____
                      _____
                      _____

 _____
                      _____
                      _____

 _____
                      _____
                      _____

 _____
                      _____
                      _____

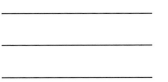

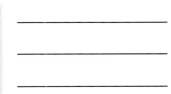

6  **Now work with a
   partner and say.**

Do you clean your bedroom?

Yes, sometimes!

7  **Make your own picture dictionary.
   Draw and write home words.**

bedroom   drink

Language lab 1

GRAMMAR 1: SHE'S COOKING

> I will talk about actions using **is / isn't ...ing.**

1 ▷ 082 Watch. Then match.

1 Leo is ●   ● a washing the car.

2 Anna is ●   ● b doing math homework.

3 Mom is ●   ● c making a cake.

4 Dad is ●   ● d drawing.

5 Grandma is ●   ● e cleaning the living room.

6 Grandpa is ●   ● f cooking.

The answer to the math problem is _____ .

Mom's cooking.

Dad **isn't cooking.** He's making a salad.

The cat **is drinking.** It's drinking water.

2 Write He's/He isn't, She's/She isn't, or It's/It isn't.

1 _____ eating. _____ sleeping.

2 _____ cooking. _____ cleaning.

3 _____ watching a movie. _____ doing her homework.

3 Now play the *Memory* Game.

> Is the rabbit sleeping?

> No, it's eating!

4 Look and read. Write yes or no.

1   The girl is jumping.   _____

2   The boy is drinking water.   _____

3   The dad is eating soup.   _____

4   The cat is washing its face. _____

5 Choose and write. Then complete the drawings.

> making   looking for

1   He's _____ a pencil.

2   She's _____ a salad.

6 Play *Do what I say*. Tell your friends what to do.

Sam   Lucy   Ella

Ella is making a cake.

Sam is sleeping.

Lucy is looking for her socks!

Story lab
READING

I will read a story about everyday activities.

1 083 🗨 **Read and listen. Where is Tom?**

I'm looking for Tom!

1 Tom's going to the castle today.

Bye-bye Tom!

2 This is the bedroom.

It's very big! It's great!

3 This is the kitchen.

Look! He's cooking!

4 This is the bathroom.

There isn't a shower!

2 Look at the story again and complete the sentences.

1   The bedroom is very _____ .

2   There _____ a shower in the bathroom.

3   Leo is _____ for Tom.

4   Tom is in the _____ .

5   Tom is _____ .

5 This is the living room.

Where's Tom?

I don't know!

6 I'm looking for Tom.

7 He's here!

Oh, he's naughty! He's playing in the bedroom.

8 He isn't playing! He's sleeping!

3 Count and write.

MATH ZONE

Castle Town Castle is very big!

There are **nine** bedrooms.

There are **two** kitchens.

There is **five** bathrooms.

There are **four** living rooms.

How many rooms are there? _____

4 Act out the story in groups.

Phonics lab
WH AND F

1 **Listen and repeat. Then write wh or f.**

1 ___ite   2 ___eel   3 ___ich   4 ___at   5 ___an   6 ___unny

2 **Listen and chant.**

Which wheel? Which wheel?

The white wheel!

The white wheel!

Which wheel?

The white wheel!

Five, fat fish

Five fat, fish

Five, funny fat fish!

4 **Listen and play the game.**

wh = arms out

f = arms front

3 **Make five fat fish.**

Experiment lab

SCIENCE: BIODEGRADABLE TRASH

I will learn about good and bad trash.

1 Listen and read.

We have trash in our homes. Some trash changes. It goes into the earth again. This trash is called biodegradable. Fruit, wood, and paper are biodegradable.

Some trash doesn't change. It is not good for our world. Plastic is not biodegradable.

We can choose what we have in our homes. We can choose what we throw away.

Can you say it? biodegradable

2 Look and check ☑ or cross ☒.

Biodegradable = ☑

Not biodegradable = ☒

 ☐  ☐  ☐

3 What is compost? What biodegradable things can you put in it? Think and write.

_____

_____

_____

EXPERIMENT TIME

How long does it take for trash to change?

1 Put soil and water on the bags.

2 Look at the bags and circle.

1 week	change / no change	change / no change
6 weeks	change / no change	change / no change

 Watch a video about trash.

Language lab 2

GRAMMAR 2: IT'S HER HOUSE.

I will talk about objects and belongings using 's.

1  **Complete the questions and answers.**
Use phrases from the box.

Laura

Fred

1 Whose pizza is it? It's Laura_____
pizza. It's her pizza.

2 W_____ water is it? It's
F_____ water. It's h_____ water.

Whose is it? It's ...'s.

This is Amy. This is **her** house.

Whose house is it?

It's Amy**'s** house.

2 Whose box is it? Write It's Elsa's or It's Tom's and circle.

Elsa

Tom

3 Play *What's the same?*
What's different?

My bag is blue. Maria's bag
is red. They're different.

CODE CRACKER

1 It's red. _____

It's blue. _____

Their boxes are the same / different .

2 It has toys and books. _____

It has books. _____

Their boxes are the same / different .

3 It's heavy. _____

Their boxes are the same / different .

Look at my photos!

COMMUNICATION

I will talk about family activities in my house.

1 📟 088 **Read and circle. Then listen and check your answers.**

Whose bathroom / kitchen is this?

Whose bedroom / house is it?

It's my Dad's / brother's .

This is our kitchen. Mom's / Dad's cooking. My sister's reading / helping .

It's a great / bad bedroom!

2 Choose and write the answers.

kicking   compost   yard   cooking

This is our _____ .
My dad's making _____ .
My grandpa's _____ .
My sister's _____ a ball.

3 Now talk about the picture with a partner.

Values Respond kindly and with interest.

4 Match. Then check the sentences that say kind things.

1 That's ●   ● a   brother is funny! ☐

2 I like ●   ● b   like his house! ☐

3 Your ●   ● c   great. ☐

4 I don't ●   ● d   your house! ☐

5 🧭 💬 **Show your partner photos of your home. Say kind things about the pictures.**

Your bedroom is great!

PROJECT AND REVIEW

 Design a dream house

Step 1

Research

 What kind of house do I want to design?

☐ Look at pictures and read books for ideas.

☐ Think about who is living in the house.

☐ Think about where the house is.

I like the ocean.

I want a horse in my yard!

Step 2

Plan

 Which rooms will I include?

☐ Think about the different rooms in a house.

☐ Make a list of your favorite activities and decide where you want to do these activities.

☐ Draw a plan of your dream house.

This my dream house. It has a swimming pool. Swimming is my favorite sport!

My sister likes to draw. In my dream house, she has an art room.

Step 3

Create

How can I create my dream house?

- [ ] Make your dream house.
- [ ] Label the model or the drawing.
- [ ] Write about the rooms.

I'm making a house. It's made of wood!

It looks fantastic. How many bedrooms are there?

There are three. I'm painting my dream home.

Step 4

Show and tell

Present your dream home.

This is my mom and dad's bedroom. There's a box of books! My mom and dad like reading.

It's great! I like your dream house!

Find interesting houses in your town.

Now I can ...

- ... use house and activity words.
- ... talk about actions using **is / isn't ...ing**.
- ... talk about objects using **'s**.
- ... talk about family activities in my house.

8 Our world

How can I create a nature scrapbook?

1 Look at the picture. How do you feel? Circle and say.

I don't like it!   It's great!   It's okay.

2 Stick the items on the picture.

3 Where do you look? Write a and b. Then say. You can add your own ideas.

a

b

1   I look up. ☐   2   I look down. ☐

4 🔊 089 **Listen and point. Then sing along and dance.**

SONG 🎵 TIME

Climb up!

🎵 tree

The **trees** are green.
The sky is blue.
I'm having fun in the trees with you!

Climb **up**, climb up,
Climb up, climb very high!
Don't look **down**,
Look, look at the sky!

The trees are high.
The sky is, too.
I'm having fun in the trees with you!

climb up

look down

one hundred and twenty-one 121

Are you up in a tree?

VOCABULARY

I will learn nature and direction words.

1 Listen, point, and repeat.

1 hill

2 bridge

3 tree

4 flower

5 path

6 forest

7 rock

8 left

9 right

10 up

11 down

12 straight

2 Look and read. Put a check ☑ or cross ☒ in the box.

1  This is a hill. ☐

2  This is a tree. ☐

3  This is a path. ☐

4  This is a forest. ☐

5  This is a bridge. ☐

3 Label the picture. Use the words from 1.

1 _____

2 _____

3 _____

4 _____

5 _____

6 _____

7 _____

4 Look at 3. Read. Then write the correct words.

1 The boy is walking **down** the hill. _____

2 The girl is climbing **up** the tree. _____

3 The dog **isn't** running straight. _____

4 The man is going **left**. _____

5 The woman is going **right**. _____

6 There are six **yellow** flowers. _____

5 🎧 091 💬 Now listen, check, and say the sentences.

The boy is walking up the hill.

6 Make your own picture dictionary. Add any nature words you know.

flower

forest

Language lab 1

> I will understand and give instructions.

1 ▶ 092 **Watch. Then choose and write.**

Milly   Leo   Mrs. Hay's

1   Anna and _____ are going to _____ farm.

2   _____ has a brother and sister.

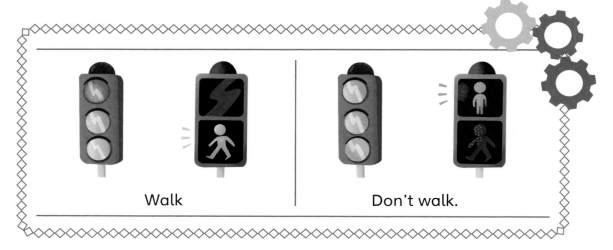

Walk   Don't walk.

2 💡 **Where is she going? Read and draw the correct path ↘.**

1   Go straight.

2   Turn left.

3   Turn right.

4   Don't turn left. Turn right.

5   Go straight.

6   Don't turn right. Turn left.

7   Turn right. Stop.

The girl is going to the _____ .

3 Look at 2 again. Now complete the directions to the other place.

1 _____ straight. ↑

2 _____ right. →

3 _____ left. ←

4 _____ _____ right. _____ left. ←

5 _____ straight. ↑

6 _____ _____ _____ . Turn right. →

7 _____ left. _____ . ←

The girl is going to the _____ .

4 Listen and read. Then listen again and dance.

CODE CRACKER

Turn left!
Turn right!
Jump!
Stop!
Don't dance!

Turn left!
Turn right!
Jump!
Don't stop!
Jump, jump, jump!
Stop!

5 Create a dance for your friends. Use these words.

kick jump run dance stop turn walk

Don't stop!

Turn left!

Story lab
READING

1  **Read and listen. Circle the new word.**

a forest   a bridge   a trampoline

2 Look at the story. Circle T (True) or F (False).

1 The children climb up. T / F

2 Miss Kelly climbs on the bridge. T / F

3 Mrs. Hay has lots of food. T / F

4 Milly jumps down. T / F

5 They all jump on the trampoline. T / F

Values Show concern for each other.

3 Who is helping Milly? Read and check ☑ or cross ☒ .

1 This is an amazing forest! ☐

2 Get the trampoline! ☐

3 I can see our school! ☐

4 Act out the story in groups. How do you help your friends?

Phonics lab

S, SH, J, AND CH

1 🔊 095 Listen and repeat. Then write **s** or **sh**.

1 _____oup

2 _____un

3 _____oe

4 _____ell

2 🔊 096 Listen and repeat. Then write **j** or **ch**.

1 _____ump

2 _____uice

3 _____icken

4 _____erry

3 🔊 097 💬 Listen and chant.

Chicken and **cheese**
and **juice** in the **shop**.
Soup in the **shop**,
Shells in the **shop**!

4 ✳ Make shell shapes.

Paint the shapes.

You can use pasta!

Put it on the refrigerator.

Stick a magnet.

5 🔊 098 Listen and play the game.

s = left   j = up

sh = right   ch = down

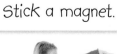

Experiment lab

SCIENCE: LANDFORMS

1 Listen and read. Then label the picture.

mountain   tectonic plate

1 _____

2 _____

Land is made of rocks. There are many different rocks of different colors. Hills and mountains are made of rocks.

There are rocks under the earth. These rocks are called tectonic plates.

2 Count and write how many layers. Then ask and answer.

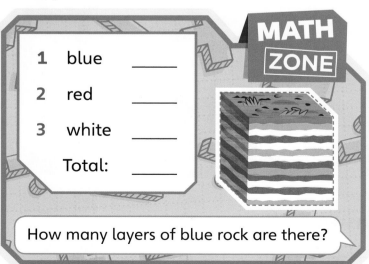

1 blue   _____

2 red   _____

3 white   _____

Total: _____

MATH ZONE

How many layers of blue rock are there?

EXPERIMENT TIME

How are mountains made?

1 Make mountains with towels.

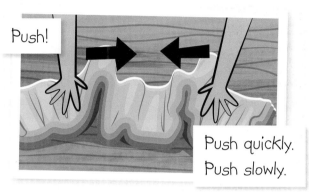

Push!

Push quickly.
Push slowly.

2 Check ☑ or cross ☒ .

1 I push and the towels …

go up ☐

go down ☐

look like mountains ☐

2 I think …

tectonic plates move ☐

tectonic plates make mountains, hills, and volcanoes ☐

▷ Watch a video about rocks.

I will use words to describe where things are.

1 Where are they? Read and check ☑ or cross ☒.

1   The gray and red bird is behind the tree. ☐

2   The brown bird is in the tree. ☐

3   The white bird is above the tree. ☐

4   The black bird is opposite the tree. ☐

5   The red and brown bird is near the tree. ☐

6   The purple bird is near the tree. ☐

2 Look. Then write.

in front of   under   on

1   The rabbit is _____ the tree.

2   The frog is _____ the flower.

3   The lizard is _____ the rock.

3 Look at 1 and 2. Ask and answer with a partner.

Where's the blue bird?

It's behind the tree.

Draw a forest!

COMMUNICATION

I will understand and give instructions to play a game.

1 Listen and check ☑ the correct picture.

2 Play *Guess which picture.*

Is the duck under the bridge?

Picture a!

No, it isn't.

3 Now listen. Then draw.

CODE CRACKER ⚙⚙

4 Choose and complete the sentences. Then tell your partner what to draw.

Use these words.

hill path forest tree
bridge flower

1 Draw a _____

2 Draw a _____

3 The _____ is next to /
in front of / under / on /
behind / above /
near the _____ .

PROJECT AND REVIEW

Make a nature scrapbook

Step 1

Research

> What things from nature can you see in your town or country?

- [ ] Write down where they are or …
- [ ] … find out where they are.
- [ ] List things you see every day.
- [ ] Learn their names.

What's this flower?

It's a tulip.

Step 2

Plan

> How can I start my nature scrapbook?

- [ ] Decide what to put in your scrapbook.
- [ ] Choose how many pages you need for trees, birds, and flowers.
- [ ] Decide what photos you want and what things you will draw.

Write about …
- What it is
- Where it is
- Why I like it

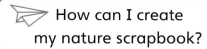

Step 3

Create

✈ How can I create my nature scrapbook?

☐ Stick or draw pictures.

☐ Write about the pictures.

☐ Write where you can see natural things and why you like them.

Amazing rocks in Hunan, China.

Step 4

Show and tell

✈ Share your work and ideas with friends.

I like that idea!

Thank you.

Where is that flower?

It's behind my house! I like the colors!

+

Look out for flowers, birds, and trees when you travel to school. Count how many you see.

Now I can ...

... use nature and direction words.

... give and understand instructions.

... describe where things are using **next to, behind, in front of**.

... understand and give instructions to play a game.

1 102 **Listen and follow. Say the number.**

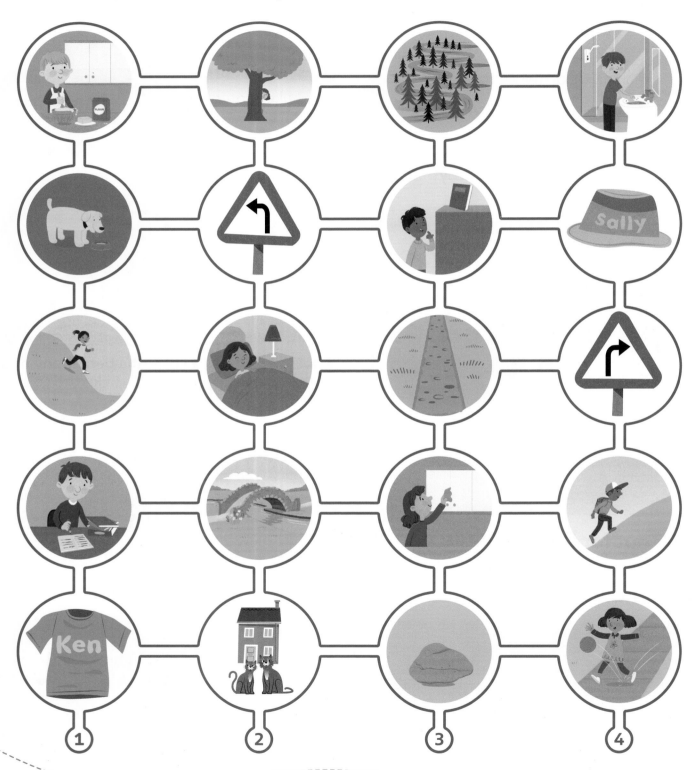

1 2 3 4

2 Read and follow. Draw the arrows. ← → ↑ ↓

1   Turn right.   ◯

The path is straight.   ◯

He's looking for a book.   ◯

Whose hat is it? It's Sally's hat.   ◯

He's in the bathroom.

2   There are flowers next to the bridge.   ◯

She's sleeping in the bedroom.   ◯

Turn left.   ◯

The dog is drinking.   ◯

He's making a cake in the kitchen.

3 Follow the arrows. Choose and write.

bathroom   right   forest
behind   Sally's

rock   in front of   sleeping
isn't   straight

1   Is she sitting _____ a tree? Yes, she is! →

There's a path in the _____ . →

He's in the _____ . ↓

Whose hat is it? It's _____ hat. ↓

Turn _____ .

2   The cats are _____ the house. →

Look at the _____ ! ↑

She _____ making a cake. She's cleaning. ↑

The path is _____ . ←

She's _____ in the bedroom.

4 💬 Ask and answer with a partner.

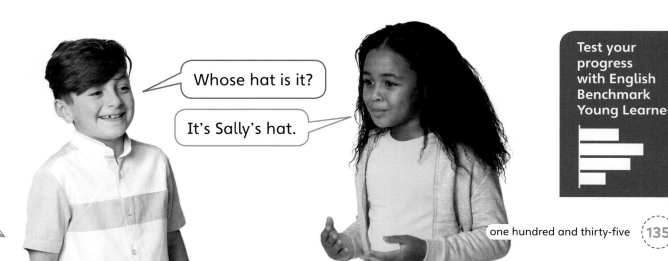

Whose hat is it?

It's Sally's hat.

Test your progress with English Benchmark Young Learners

Beautiful gardens
CULTURE

1 🗨 Look at the pictures. What places can you see? Say.

2 📞 Listen and read.

Wow! It's a secret garden! It's very old!

The Lost Gardens of Heligan

The Lost Gardens of Heligan are very old. They are in Cornwall, England.

The gardens are beautiful now. There are giants in the gardens! The giants are made of rock.

Let's make it beautiful again!

This is a giant's head! Look at its hair. It's made of leaves and grass.

This giant is watching something!

This giant is tired. It's sleeping!

Singapore—the Garden City!

Fun Fact! You can grow plants on walls!

Singapore is a big city. There are lots of beautiful gardens. Many people live in apartments, and they don't have gardens or yards. But some people grow flowers on roofs and on walls. Plants, trees, and flowers make cities look beautiful, and they make oxygen.

3 Choose and complete.

walls   rocks   trees

1   There are giants made of _____ in the garden in Cornwall.

2   You can grow plants on _____ !

3   Plants, _____ , and flowers make our cities beautiful.

4  Talk to a partner about the gardens.

I like the garden on the roof!

Me, too!
It looks fresh and green!

My Culture

Find out about interesting gardens
in your country.

5 Design and make a garden in a pot.

1   Put earth in a flower pot.

2   Add stones and small flowers
and plants.

3   You can have a castle, a house,
a river, or a bridge in your garden.

6 Describe your garden in a pot.

This is my garden pot. It has
purple flowers and a bridge!

Wordlist

Welcome Unit

Days of the Week Vocabulary
Monday
Tuesday
Wednesday
Thursday
Friday
Saturday
Sunday

Months Vocabulary
January
February
March
April
May
June
July
August
September
October
November
December

Seasons Vocabulary
Spring
Summer
Fall
Winter

Unit 1

Places Vocabulary
café
castle
farm
house

library
museum
park
playground
river
school
store
swimming pool

Phonics lab
bag
cap
cat
leg
man
mat
pan
clap
pen
peg
pet
ten
wet

Experiment lab
bricks
cement
spaghetti
steel
straws
strong
tower
wood

Unit 2

Animals Vocabulary
bat
cow
donkey
goat

owl
porcupine

Daily Routine Vocabulary
brush my teeth
eat
go to school
sleep
wake up
wash my face

Phonics lab
dog
fox
hop
hot
jog
frog
stop
bin
hit
sing
sit
win
six

Experiment lab
day
earth
hours
months
night
shines
sky
sun
year

Culture lab

Antarctica
Arctic
bears
December
elephant seals
elks
June
Kiruna
lights
moon
river
snowmobile
sun
Sweden
town
wood

Unit 3

Adjectives for Objects Vocabulary

clean
dirty
gold
hard
heavy
light
new
old
round
silver
soft
square

Phonics lab

bug
nut
run
sun
rug

jug
six
taxi
box
fox
ox
ax

Experiment lab

liquid
rock
shape
solid
waterfall

Unit 4

Adjectives for People and Feelings Vocabulary

angry
friendly
funny
happy
helpful
kind
lazy
naughty
sad
shy
tired
young

Phonics lab

jacket
jaguar
jar
jeans
jog
juice
jump
jungle

yak
yellow
yes
yo-yo
yogurt
you
young
yours

Experiment lab

eyebrows
eyes
face
muscles
mouths
noses
artist
yawn

Culture lab

bagpipes
blow
drums
flute
India
instrument
Japan
neck
pipes
Scotland
sticks
strings
traditional
veena

Wordlist

Unit 5

Food and Drink Vocabulary
bread
cheese
chicken
cookies
fish
ice cream
juice
pasta
rice
salad
soup
water

Phonics lab
chair
cheese
cherries
chess
chicken
chips
sheep
shelf
ship
shirt
shoes
shop
shorts

Experiment lab
almonds
coconuts
farmer
combine harvester
factory

ice cream
milk
nuts
pick
plants
soybeans
vanilla
healthy
machine

Unit 6

Sports Vocabulary
basketball
catch
hit
jump
kick
run
soccer
table tennis
team
throw
volleyball
watch

Phonics lab
thank
that
there
these
they
thing
thirteen
this
those
three
throw

Experiment lab
air
blow
court
far
field
important
centimeters
lungs
match
measure
measuring
meter
net

Culture lab
China
dragon
flag
festival
gold cup
gondola
hitting
Italy
leaves
race
regatta
rice
tail
teams
Venice
winner
Yueyang
Zongzi

Unit 7

Daily Routine Vocabulary
clean
cook
do homework
drink
look for
bake a cake
take a shower

Rooms Vocabulary
bathroom
bedroom
living room
kitchen
yard

Phonics lab
fan
farm
fat
fish
five
funny
what
wheel
when
where
which
white

Experiment lab
biodegradable
compost
paper
plastic
soil
throw away
trash

Unit 8

Directions Vocabulary
down
left
right
straight
up

Natural World Vocabulary
bridge
cloud
flower
forest
hill
path
tree

Phonics lab
cheese
cherry
chicken
jeep
juice
jump
see
shell
shoe
shop
soup
sun

Experiment lab
hills
land
landforms
layers
mountains
push
rocks
tectonic plates
towels
volcanoes

Culture lab
beautiful
Cornwall
England
fresh
garden
giants
grass
oxygen
roof
secret
Singapore
walls

Continents
Africa
Antarctica
Asia
Australia
Europe
North America
South America

Grammar Reference

Unit 1

Grammar 1

Present Simple with *like* (affirmative, negative, and question form):

I *like* cats. I *don't like* frogs.
He *likes* dogs.
She *doesn't like* birds.

Does Tom *like* horses?
Yes, he does./
No, he doesn't.

Grammar 2

There's/There are ...

There*'s* a mouse.   There *are* frogs.
There *isn't* a rabbit.   There *aren't* any fish.

Unit 2

Grammar 1

Present Simple for routines and general truths (affirmative, negative, and question form):

I go to the park. *I don't go* to school.
We play soccer. *We don't play* music.
You eat in the café. *You don't eat* in the car.
They go to the store. *They don't go* to the farm.

On Saturdays, *do you go* to school? No, I don't.

Do you play soccer? Yes, I do.

Grammar 2

Present Simple for routines and general truths (affirmative, negative, and question form):

She eats a banana every day.
He doesn't ride his bike every day.

Does he swim every day?
Yes, *he does.* No, *he doesn't.*

Unit 3

Grammar 1

Possessives: my/mine, your/yours, his/his, her/hers

Whose is it?
It's *mine*. *My* hat is red.

Whose is it?
It's *yours*. *Your* coat is new.

It's *hers*. *Her* bag is heavy.
It's *his*. *His* sweater is dirty.

Grammar 2

Possessives: our/ours, their/theirs

It's *ours*. *Our* ball is green.
It's *theirs*. *Their* book is old.

Unit 4

Grammar 1

***be* verb (third person affirmative, negative, and question form):**

Is he angry?
No, he *isn't*. He*'s* tired.

Is she shy?
Yes, she *is*.

Is she sad?
No, she *isn't*.

Adverbs of frequency: always/sometimes/never

She *is always* shy.
He *is sometimes* tired.
She *is never* naughty.

Grammar 2

***Have* for possession (question form):**

Do you have a lizard?
Yes, *I do*.

Do you have a goat?
No, *I don't*.

It's and *its*

It's my lizard! *It's* friendly. *Its* tail is green.
Its eyes are orange. *It's* never angry.

Grammar Reference

Unit 5

Grammar 1

Can for permission (question form and natural answers):

Can I have some building blocks, please?
Sure!

Can I have a pear, please?
Sorry, no!

Grammar 2

Can for permission (question form with this/ that for proximity):

Can I have **this** book, please?
This one?
Yes!

Can I have **that** ball, please?
That one?
Yes!

Can I have a teddy bear, please?
This one or *that* one?
This one!

Unit 6

Grammar 1

Present Progressive (first person affirmative statements, questions, and short form answers):

I'm eating.

You're sleeping.

Are you drinking water?
Yes, *I am.*

Are you running?
No, *I'm not.*

Grammar 2

Can for ability (question form)

Can you fly?
Yes, I *can.*

Can you climb trees?
No, I *can't.*

Unit 7

Grammar 1

Present Progressive (third person singular affirmative and negative statements):

Dad *is cooking* pasta.
He *isn't eating*.
Mom *isn't watching* a movie.

She*'s reading* a book.
The dog *is jumping*.
It *isn't sleeping*.

Present Progressive (third person singular question and answer forms):

Is he throwing a ball?
Yes, *he is*.

Is she doing homework?
No, *she isn't*.

Grammar 2

Possessive 's:

Whose book is it?
It's Mom*'s*.

Whose hat is it?
It's Dad*'s*.

Unit 8

Grammar 1

Imperatives:

Go straight.

Don't go straight.

Turn left.

Don't turn right.

Grammar 2

Preposition of place:

The ball is *under* the table.
The doll is *next to* the box.
The eraser is *on* the shelf.
The car is *in front of* the ball.
The teddy bear is *in* the box.
The hat is *behind* the box.
The book is *near* the eraser.
The ball is *opposite* the doll.
The train is *above* the eraser.

Irregular verbs

	Present Simple	Past Simple
be	I am You are He/She/It is We are They are	I was You were He/She/It was We were They were
be able to	I can You can He/She/It can We can They can	I could You could He/She/It could We could They could
draw	I draw You draw He/She/It draws We draw They draw	I drew You drew He/She/It drew We drew They drew
drink	I drink You drink He/She/It drinks We drink They drink	I drank You drank He/She/It drank We drank They drank
eat	I eat You eat He/She/It eats We eat They eat	I ate You ate He/She/It ate We ate They ate
go	I go You go He/She/It goes We go They go	I went You went He/She/It went We went They went
have	I have You have He/She/It has We have They have	I had You had He/She/It had We had They had

	Present Simple	Past Simple
make	I make You make He/She/It makes We make They make	I made You made He/She/It made We made They made
run	I run You run He/She/It runs We run They run	I ran You ran He/She/It ran We ran They ran
sing	I sing You sing He/She/It sings We sing They sing	I sang You sang He/She/It sang We sang They sang
sleep	I sleep You sleep He/She/It sleeps We sleep They sleep	I slept You slept He/She/It slept We slept They slept
swim	I swim You swim He/She/It swims We swim They swim	I swam You swam He/She/It swam We swam They swam
throw	I throw You throw He/She/It throws We throw They throw	I threw You threw He/She/It threw We threw They threw
wake	I wake You wake He/She/It wakes We wake They wake	I woke You woke He/She/It woke We woke They woke

OUR WORLD

INTRO:

Here we stand: children of every age,
This is our world and the world's our stage.
We can laugh, we can cry — we can float, we can fly,
We can dance, we can sing — we can do almost anything
in OUR world ... our *beautiful* world.

VERSE 1:

Some of us are small; some of us are tall,
Some of us are shy; some of us say hi to everybody,
Some of us like numbers; some of us love words,
Some of us watch football, and some of us watch the birds!

(CHORUS)

This is *our* world ... we're different but the same.
We live and learn together — we get to know each other ...
in OUR world ... our *beautiful* world.

VERSE 2:

Some of us like music; some of us like cars,
Some of us draw pictures, looking at the stars,
Some of us are scientists, trying to find the code,
All of us can help a friend and give a hand to hold.

This is *our* world — there's room for everyone.
We learn to live together, and we have a lot of fun ...
In **our** world ... in **our** world ... in our beautiful world!

Pearson Education Limited
KAO TWO
KAO Park
Hockham Way
Harlow, Essex
CM17 9SR
England

and Associated Companies throughout the world.

english.com/englishcode

First published 2021

ISBN: 978-1-292-35225-1

Set in Heinemann Roman 13pt

Printed in Slovakia by Neografia

Acknowledgements

The publishers and author(s) would like to thank the following people and institutions for their feedback and comments during the development of the material:

Mexico

Clara Eugenia Krauze De Orellana (Centro Educatvo Moderna), Erika Alejandra Vazquez Limon (Colegio Keppler), Liliana Hernandez Mercado (Instituto Ovalle Monday), Aldo Javier Inclan Aragon (Ctec), Daniela Jaqueline Martinez Carsolio (Colegio Carsolio), Gloria Mariana Bonilla Vargas (Universidad Panamericana), Jaqueline Suzanne Torres Contreras (Universidad Mexicana), Blanca Estela Cadena Martinez (Colegio Elena Jackson), Maria Luisa Leslie Miranda Sanciprian (Colegio Maria Montessori), Yanequeo Melchor Rosas (The Lord Bertrand Russell School), Fernando Javier Sanchez Machado (Crandon Institute), Catalina Graciela Eljure Vaca (Instituto Cultural (Mixto)), Mayely Fabiola López Kanagúsico (Highland Enterprise Education, S.C.), Paulina Sanchez (Colegio Atenea), Marlene Correa Canto (Colegio Privado), Fabiola Carmona González (Colegio Ityc), Natalia Castillo Ruiz (Colegio Victoria Tepeyac), Colegio Cristobal Colón, LA Sale, Escuela morales, Instituto Emilian, Colegio Benavente, Colegio Alamas, Colegio Franco Español, Centro de Aprendizaje Piaget, Instituto Ingles Mexican, The Lord Bertrand Russell School.

China

Ryan Kittel (American Baby International Education), 江超逸 (V-Ron English)

Image Credits:

123RF.com: andresr 68, Anne Jose Kan 29, bogumil 12, erstudiostok 26, lianem 122, lizon 82, Natallia Khlapushyna 118, Olga Popova 46, PaylessImages 35, Petr Joura 114, Sergey Novikov 90, talanis 90, Vadim Georgiev 10, Wavebreak Media Ltd 36, 64; **Alamy Stock Photo:** ClickAlps 40, Dorling Kindersley 73, Jeremy Trew, Trewimage 20, Kevin Schafer 136, KeyWorded 72, nobleIMAGES 136, Radhakrishnan Valappil 72, Ryan Deberardinis 22, Sergey Novikov 58, Tetra Images 108, Wothan 72; **Bridgeman Images:** 60; **Getty Images:** 4uda4ka 68, ALEAIMAGE 47, Altinosmanaj 58, Andyd 85, apomares 88, Ariel Skelley 35, Artem Hvozdkov 05/04/2020, Azure-Dragon 76, bazilfoto 25, beastfromeast 69, Becart 60, bee32 37, benedek 15, Bill Oxford 12, BLOOM image 35, Boogich 51, Chefmd 108, Choreograph 27, cjp 115, Construction Photography/Avalon 106/107, damircudic 26, Dena Hurlebaus 37, DGLimages 119, Dmitrii Balabanov 19, Don Bishop 56, drbimages 128, eAlisa 32, Eddie Granlund/Folio Images 40, ExperienceInteriors 108, FaST_9 29, fcafotodigital 64, FooTToo 122, fotostorm 22, gedzun 64, GK Hart/Vikki Hart 24, GlobalP 25, 163, 163, GoodLifeStudio 15, hanohiki 23, Hybrid Images 108, iEverest 56, ImageDB 82, Imgorthand 22, 23, 69, ismagilov 56/57, James Harwood II, Jasper Cole 133, JGI/Jamie Grill 26, JMichl 83, JohnGollop 18, JohnnyGreig 26, Jose Luis Pelaez Inc 58, Jupiterimages 32, 60, Karthik Arumugam 26, Kenishirotie 122, kivoart 85, Kontrec 18, kostman 87, Kraig Scarbinsky 108, Kristian Bell 42/43, Kwanchai_Khammuean 27, Ljupco 90, Lubo Ivanko 29, magda_rzymanek 58, malerapaso 115, Manish 51, Martin Wahlborg 15, michaeljung 64, Mima Foto / EyeEm 18, 38, 78, 91, 102, MoniqueRodriguez 97, monkeybusinessimages 12, 32, 35, Nataliia Pyzhova 58, nechaev-kon 50, Nerthuz 50, Nick David 67, 67, 67, Nik_Merkulov 50, nikkytok 12, OkinawaPottery 92, oliverscott-ison 18, Olivier Renck 92, omgimages 12, 133, Onzeg 108, Per Eriksson 40, Peter Cade 19, PHOTOSTOCK-ISRAEL/Science Photo Library 28, pkanchana 50, polarica 56, Portra 117, Ridofranz 93, Ron Levine 90, RTimages 18, Ruben Earth 41, sayhmog 82, SDI Productions 101, SeventyFour 69, shinichi.imanaka 57, skodonnell 76, skynesher 93, SolStock 28, 35, 58, South_agency 90, Stockbyte 51, 64, stockstudioX 120/121, Svetlana Mokrova 24/25, 24, SylvieBouchard 40, Tarzhanova 55, Tetra Images - Daniel Grill 22, The Sydney Morning Herald 74/75, Tom Merton 58, travellinglight 85, Tyson1 37, ULTRA.F 58, unalozmen 11, Vacl 11, ValeriKimbro 32, vfoto 76, vichie81

40, Watcharapol_Kun 24, Westend61 21, winyuu 17, Wladimir Bulgar/Science Photo Library 11, yalcinsonat1 82, Yasser Chalid 108, Yinjia Pan 25, yipengge 122, zhengzaishuru 19, zlikovec 122; **Pearson Education Ltd:** Jon Barlow 4, 5, 10, 11, 21, 24, 25, 27, 34, 35, 37, 39, 42, 43, 45, 52, 55, 56, 57, 59, 60, 67, 71, 74, 75, 77, 79, 85, 88, 89, 91, 93, 96, 103, 105, 106, 107, 109, 114, 117, 120, 121, 123, 128, 135, Jules Selmes 19, Silverpin Design Company Ltd 111; **Shutterstock.com:** 69, Aaron Amat 58, Africa Studio 27, 79, 99, Air Images 99, Alex Chernyavsky 41, Alis Leonte 15, All for you friend 46, Anastasiya Stoma 51, Andriy Solovyov 26, Anna Photographer 12, 22, 36, 38, 100, 102, 130, Antonina Potapenko 108, Artazum and Iriana Shiyan 12, bogumil 92, Brian Yarvin 104, CapturePB 54, Christophe Testi 97, Cocos.Bounty 118, Coprid 18, CroMary 93, Dabarti CGI 19, Dan76 137, DenisNata 76, 111, Denys Prykhodov. 35, Dimitris Leonidas 55, Dmitry Naumov 12, Don Mammoser 26, Dzarek 115, elenovsky 46, Eric Isselee 64, Erkki Alvenmod 40, Evgeny Karandaev 85, fiphoto 82, Fotokostic 90, 90, 90, frantic00 90, GCapture 97, George Rudy 117, Goodluz 118, Halfpoint 87, Here 92, Horst Petzold 82, Hung Chung Chih 26, 133, hxdbzxy 27, Ievgen Shapovalov 26, IM_VISUALS 19, Independent birds 28, 163, Ingrid Prats 6, 6, 6, 6, irik V 11, Ivan Kuzmin 26, JaySi 90, Jeff McGraw 32, Joy Brown 83, Jukka Jantunen 29, Julia Kuznetsova 133, Just dance 50, Kapi Ng 12, kazoka 17, keerati 11/10/2020, kittirat roekburi 12, Konstantin Faraktinov 85, 85, Konstantin Gushcha 18, Kozlik 17, LeNi 76, Littlekidmoment 92, Lopolo 26, Lordn 9, Lukas Gojda 9, 12, 14, 18, 22, 27, 27, 31, 32, 36, 38, 44, 65, 76, 77, 78, 81, 82, 86, 91, 94, 99, 100, 102, 103, 108, 111, 118, 122, 123, 125, 126, 130, 131, 132, 135, LumineImages 58, lunamarina 58, M. Unal Ozmen 76, madmonkey0328 29, ManeeshUpadhyay 128, MaraZe 76, Mark Agnor 83, Max Topchii 82, Michael Warwick 12, Mistervlad 113, MNStudio 83, mskova 68, myboys.me 108, Nataliia Melnychuk 28, Nataly Studio 47, New Africa 32, Nice to meet you 15, Nigmatulina Aleksandra 119, Oksana Kuzmina 64, oksana2010 76, OlgaGi 46, orxy 51, Palokha Tetiana 97, Phillip Dyhr Hobbs 18, PHOTOMDP 104, Poznyakov 68, 118, PRESSLAB 111, Pressmaster 61, Prophotoo 15, Provasilich 47, Purino 92, pzAxe 69, R. Gino Santa Maria 115, Radomir Rezny 122, Robbi 22, Roman Sigaev 64, Romix Image 104, Ronnachai Palas 104, Room27 108, RoongsaK 118, Sam's Studio 136, Sean Locke Photography 128, Sergey Novikov 90, 99, 100, Shi Yali 104, skodonnell 133, smereka 26, SmLyubov 55, Sophie Leguil 136, SpeedKingz 90, Stanislav Glushko 19, stocker1970 122, Stor24 12, Suslik1983 117, Sveta Lagutina 65, Svitlana-ua 128, Syda Productions 32, 69, 100, Taigi 117, Tatyana Vyc 108, tcharts 24/25, teekayu 28, 37, Teresa Kasprzycka 132, timquo 17, 21, 32, 35, 36, 54, 86, 93, 96, Tobik 76, topseller 93, Tracy Whiteside 36, urfin 76, VaLiza 108, Viacheslav Lopatin 19, vidguten 12, Vladimir Konstantinov 29, Vladvm 18, vvoe 55, wavebreakmedia 101, Yakobchuk VIiacheslav 58, Yeamake 82, Yuri Samsonov 76, Yuriy Golub 83, zebra0209 119, zhengchengbao 122, Zurijeta 114

Animation screen shots

Artwork by ACA/Sylvie Poggio Artists, production by Dardanele Studio

All other images © Pearson Education

Every effort has been made to trace the copyright holders and we apologise in advance for any unintentional omissions. We would be pleased to insert the appropriate acknowledgement in any subsequent edition of this publication.

Illustrated by: ACA/Sylvie Poggio Artists, pp. 8–9, 16–17, 30–31, 48–49, 62–63, 80–81, 94–95, 112–113, 126–127; Tim Bradford/Beehive Illustration, pp. 18 (robot), 32 (robot), 50 (robot), 64 (robot), 82 (robot), 96 (robot), 114 (robot), 128 (robot); Martyn Cain/Beehive Illustration, pp. 38 (d-e, h, l, r), 70 (a-e, g-t), 102 (a, c, e, h-q, t), 134 (a-b, d-e, g, i-j, m-o, s-t), 142–145; Laura Deo/Lemonade Illustration, pp. 7, 14, 20, 28, 34, 46–47, 52, 57, 61, 66, 78–79, 84, 92–93, 98, 110–111, 116, 124–125, 130, 136; Elaine Leggett/D'Aila Illustration Agency, p.65 (top left); John Lund/Beehive Illustration, pp. 6, 13, 18, 26, 32, 43–44, 45 (middle and bottom left), 50 (middle and bottom left), 58, 59 (top and bottom left), 64, 65 (bottom left), 76–77, 82, 86, 90–91, 96, 99, 102 (d, s), 108, 109 (top and middle), 114 (middle), 122–123, 128, 132, 134 (p); Berta Maluenda/Bright Agency, pp. 23, 27, 45 (bottom right), 50 (bottom right), 59 (bottom right), 87, 101, 109 (bottom right), 119, 131; Robyn McLennan, pp. 10–11, 24–25, 42–43, 56–57, 74–75, 88–89, 106–107, 12–121, Stickers 1 (top), Stickers 2, Stickers 3; Mark Ruffle/Beehive Illustration, pp. 4, 9, 21, 25, 33, 35, 38 (a-c, f-g, i-k, m-q, s-t), 51, 53, 65 (right), 67, 69, 70(f), 75, 83, 85, 89, 97, 102 (b,f-g, r), 107, 114 (top), 115, 117, 120, 129, 134 (c, f, h, k-l, q-r).

Cover Image: Front: **Pearson Education Ltd:** Jon Barlow